OXFORD MEDICAL PUBLICATIONS

Attempted Suicide
A practical guide to its nature and management

Attempted Suicide

A practical guide to its nature and management

Second edition

KEITH HAWTON and JOSE CATALAN
Department of Psychiatry, University of Oxford

OXFORD   NEW YORK TOKYO
OXFORD UNIVERSITY PRESS

Oxford University Press, Walton Street, Oxford OX2 6DP
Oxford New York Toronto
Delhi Bombay Calcutta Madras Karachi
Petaling Jaya Singapore Hong Kong Tokyo
Nairobi Dar es Salaam Cape Town
Melbourne Auckland
and associated companies in
Beirut Berlin Ibadan Nicosia

Oxford is a trade mark of Oxford University Press

Published in the United States
by Oxford University Press, New York

First published 1982
Reprinted with corrections 1983
Second edition 1987
Reprinted 1990

British Library Cataloguing in Publication Data
Hawton, Keith
Attempted suicide : a practical guide to its
nature and management. — 2nd ed. —
(Oxford medical publications)
1. Suicide
I. Title   II. Catalán, José
616.85'8445   RC569
ISBN 0–19–261596–3

Library of Congress Cataloging-in-Publication Data
Hawton, Keith, 1942–
Attempted suicide.
(Oxford medical publications)
Bibliography: p.
Includes index.
1. Suicide—Prevention. 2. Suicide—Psychological
aspects. 3. Crisis intervention (Psychiatry)
4. Psychotherapy, Brief. 5. Suicide—Great Britain.
I. Catalán, José, 1949–   . II. Title. III. Series.
[DNLM: 1. Crisis Intervention. 2. Suicide, Attempted.
WM 401 H399a]
RC569.H38 1987 616.85'8445 86–23502
ISBN 0–19–261596–3

Printed by Ipswich Book Company Ltd

Foreword to the first edition

JOHN BANCROFT

MRC Unit for Reproductive Biology, Edinburgh

The current epidemic of self-poisoning and self-injury presents a formidable challenge. Because it usually entails poisoning or other self-harm, the medical profession is inevitably involved and these cases create considerable demands on emergency medical services. And yet the crises and problems that lead to the overdoses cover the full range of life's difficulties, often in people who are vulnerable or ill-equipped to cope with such stresses. The basic problems are seldom medical. A conventional source of help in these circumstances is the psychiatrist and yet it is a relatively small minority of patients who are psychiatrically ill or are likely to benefit from psychiatric treatment. All too often psychiatrists select those with psychiatric illness and leave the rest as being outside their scope. But the numbers of patients, especially those who are not ill, have grown enormously.

There has been no shortage of research on the epidemiology of this behaviour. The secular trend is clear and alarming. We have good evidence of the characteristics of the self-poisoning population. But we still have very little understanding of why people behave in this way, which is fundamental to any form of primary prevention. There has also been little systematic study of how best to help people after such overdoses.

In this book, Keith Hawton and José Catalan deal with these last two issues in some depth as well as providing a useful review of the epidemiological and demographic evidence. Their principal objective is clearly to provide practical guidelines for the health professional who deals with self-poisoning and self-injury patients, and who wants to help them. There is a much wider relevance, however, as the principles of assessment and counselling described by them are applicable to most forms of crisis.

The clinical approach outlined in this book has developed over the years within the Oxford University Department of Psychiatry and, more recently, the Barnes Unit of the Radcliffe Infirmary and John Radcliffe II Hospital, Oxford. Throughout this time, there has been an extremely close link between the clinical service and clinical research, each one shaping the development of the other. The aims of the various research studies have been determined by the needs of a developing service and, for example, the method of assessing overdose patients has been strongly influenced by research experience. The advantages of such cross-fertilization are clearly evident in this highly practical book.

Acknowledgements for the first edition

We thank the many people who have enabled us to write this book. Much of the material reported here is based on findings of the Attempted Suicide Research Team in the University Department of Psychiatry in Oxford. In addition to the authors this team has at various times included the following: John Bancroft, Eileen Blackstock, Deborah Cole, Joan Fagg, Olivia Harvard-Watts, Tamsin Humphries, Breda Kingston, Pamela Marsack, Shulamit Ramon, Frankie Reynolds, Susan Simkin, Angela Skrimshire, Jean Smith, and Pat Wells. Considerable assistance with analysis of the epidemiological data has been provided by Leicester Gill of the Oxford University Unit of Clinical Epidemiology. Financial support for research projects has been received from the Department of Health and Social Security, Oxford Regional Health Authority, and the Oxford Medical Research Fund.

The approaches to assessment and brief treatment of attempted suicide patients developed out of discussion over the years with members of the clinical service working in the Barnes Unit in the Radcliffe Infirmary, and later the John Radcliffe II Hospital, Oxford. Members of this Unit have also co-operated with some of the research projects mentioned here, thus enabling them to be completed successfully. Particular thanks are due to Dr Edward Smith who, as consultant in charge of the Unit, has made available the patients that have been the focus of the research team's work.

We are indebted to John Bancroft, who took the initial responsibility for setting up both the Attempted Suicide Research Team and the Barnes Unit and who in addition made numerous helpful suggestions during the preparation of this book. The following, as representatives of various professional groups concerned with the management of attempted suicide patients, also provided invaluable comments on an earlier draft of the book: Harry Dickinson, Robert Fieldsend, Michael Gelder, Robert Litman, and Jon Margo (psychiatry); Caroline Collins, Jenny McPherson, and

Linda Whitehead (nurse counsellors); Ann Dunseath (general hospital nursing); Breda Kingston and Joan Kirk (clinical psychology); Adrian Collin (social work); and Theo Schofield (general practice). Beverley Haggis typed the manuscript of the book with care and enthusiasm. Lastly, we thank Professor A. Beck of the University of Pennsylvania for permission to reproduce his Scale of Suicidal Intent, and the editors of *Social Psychiatry* for permission to publish Figure 3.

Oxford   K. H.
January 1982   J. C.

Preface to the second edition

The positive responses to the first edition of this book, both in this country and abroad, and the extensive research work which has been published in the field of suicidal behaviour during the past five years, encouraged us to prepare this new edition. In doing so we have paid particular attention to the recent changes in the epidemiology of attempted suicide. While there have been welcome signs that the massive increase in the extent of this behaviour which occurred during the 1970s has peaked, and that there may even have been a recent decline in the numbers of people being referred to hospitals after deliberate self-poisoning or self-injury, the problem of attempted suicide remains as much of a health care problem as it was when we wrote the first edition.

The new edition includes further evidence for the likely contributory role of psychotropic drug prescribing in relation to self-poisoning. We have enlarged the sections on attempted suicide by adolescents, and the motivational aspects of self-poisoning, incorporating recent findings in these areas. The association between unemployment and attempted suicide is given more attention, especially in view of the escalation in unemployment rates in the United Kingdom during the past few years. We have not found it necessary to modify greatly the descriptions of assessment, treatment, and prevention, which form the core of this book, but have included the findings of recent research studies and their implications for clinical practice, and added a further case example illustrating treatment of an unemployed man who took an overdose. Since the appearance of the first edition, new official guidelines on the management of attempted suicide patients have appeared in this country, and they are summarized here. It is encouraging to note these new recommendations are largely along the lines that we suggested in the first edition.

The work of the attempted suicide research team in Oxford has recently been assisted by grants from the Medical Research Council and Oxford Regional Health Authority. We are grateful to those people, including colleagues and reviewers, who have made suggestions about the earlier edition, many of which have been incorporated here. Lastly, we thank the Oxford University Press for encouraging us to prepare this edition, and Caroline Fordham and Triona Baillie who have done the typing.

Oxford   K. H.
March 1986   J. C.

Contents

PART I

The nature of attempted suicide

1

Introduction

The problem of attempted suicide now poses one of the major challenges facing health care services in this and other countries. During the 1960s and 1970s, the numbers of people presenting in hospital casualty departments each year after deliberately taking overdoses or injuring themselves steadily increased. As a result, deliberate self-poisoning has become the most common reason for acute medical admission of women to hospital, and second only to heart attacks as the most common medical reason for admission of men. It has been estimated that more than 100 000 hospital admissions per year in the United Kingdom are caused by deliberate self-poisoning. This phenomenon appears to be prevalent throughout the Western world (Wexler *et al.* 1978).

Patients who take overdoses or deliberately injure themselves pose considerable strains on busy *medical* and *nursing staff* in general hospitals. The majority of such patients require admission to hospital beds which are barely sufficient in number to cope with patients with other medical conditions. The social and psychiatric problems of attempted suicide patients necessitate attention from *psychiatrists, social workers*, and other staff who are responsible for assessing such patients and providing them with help after discharge from hospital. Finally, *general practitioners* and *voluntary agencies* often have important roles to play, not only in providing aftercare, but also in dealing with the threat or possibility of attempts.

As a result of the expansion in the problem of attempted suicide, a major research effort has been directed towards investigation of the characteristics of people who deliberately poison or injure themselves. This began with the work of Stengel and Cook (1958), who studied attempted suicide in the London area. Subsequent work in Edinburgh, Oxford, Bristol, Southampton, and elsewhere in this country, as well as abroad, has added to our knowledge of

3

the problem. There is much information on the characteristics of those who make attempts, where they live, the problems they face, and the important associations between attempted suicide and suicide. We have less understanding of the reasons why the behaviour occurs. Knowledge is gradually accumulating about how best to help people who make attempts, but little headway has been made in the prevention of this behaviour. It is to these issues that this book, which is primarily a practical guide to the management of self-poisoning and self-injury patients, is particularly addressed.

Before proceeding any further, it is worth making a general point about the social meaning of attempted suicide. The nature of the act (self-inflicted harm) and its possible risks in relation to the individual's physical well-being, make the link between attempted suicides and health services inevitable. However, this does not mean that suicide attempts should be regarded as 'diseases', or those attempting it as necessarily being 'ill'. Clearly, some people making suicide attempts may suffer serious physical harm or even die as a result of the act of self-harm, and a small proportion of attempters do, indeed, have major psychiatric disorders. However, individuals who harm themselves should not generally be considered to be psychiatrically ill because of their behaviour, but rather should be seen as people made vulnerable by personal and social difficulties, and who remain responsible for their actions. The dangers inherent in adopting a medical attitude to attempted suicide are as great as those involved in the opposite extreme position, where it is considered as a form of deviant, unacceptable, or immoral behaviour deserving punishment. We hope that this book will help to clarify issues of disease and responsibility in relation to attempted suicide.

The problem of terminology must also be dealt with. The term 'attempted suicide' has been criticized because it is used to describe behaviour which, probably more often than not, lacks any serious suicidal intention. As such it is therefore a mismoner. Several other terms have been introduced as alternatives. These include, for example, 'parasuicide' (Kreitman *et al.* 1969), 'pseudocide' (Lennard-Jones and Asher 1959), and 'deliberate self-harm' (Morgan 1979). All have their drawbacks: 'parasuicide' because it also implies suicidal intentions, 'pseudocide' because it suggests mimicry of suicide, and 'deliberate self-harm' because it implies that physical harm always occurs. We do not feel strongly about the use of one term as opposed to another. 'Deliberate self-poisoning' and 'deliberate self-injury' describe the behaviour without implying any specific motive and are probably preferable. These will often be used in this book. However, because these terms are somewhat cumbersome, 'overdose' will at times be used for the sake of brevity. 'Deliberate self-poisoning' and 'overdose' are used to describe the deliberate ingestion of more than the prescribed amount of medical substances, or ingestion of substances never intended for human consumption, irrespective of whether harm was intended. Similarly, 'deliberate self-injury' has been used to describe any intentional self-inflicted injury, irrespective of the apparent purpose of the act. Where the behaviour in general is being considered, the terms 'attempted suicide' and 'suicidal behaviour' will be used for the purpose of convenience.

Because there is an increasing tendency for non-medical personnel to be involved in the management of patients after deliberate self-poisoning or self-injury, the general term 'therapist' will often be used to signify a person providing such care. In contexts where members of either sex could be involved, the convention has been adopted of using 'he' as the personal pronoun.

In preparing this book, attention has been paid to research findings from this country and abroad, although the emphasis is on the problem of attempted suicide in the United Kingdom. A research team in Oxford has been investigating various aspects of the problem since 1972, and during recent years has focused particularly on evaluating ways of providing help for patients who have made attempts. This has been possible because an experimental unit for these patients has been established in the general hospital in Oxford. Much of the information concerning assessment and treatment methods has therefore been derived from local research and clinical experience. We have often relied on clinical examples to illustrate the text. (In all cases, names and other details have been altered to preserve anonymity.) It is hoped that these examples will make it easier for the reader to become familiar with the problems and methods described. The intention throughout has been to provide practical guidance.

The main focus of the book is on how to help patients who have taken overdoses or injured themselves. In the next two chapters, the principal findings concerning the patterns of attempted suicide and the problems faced by people who make attempts will be described to provide a background for the subsequent chapters on management. The fourth chapter provides a detailed description of the assessment of patients who have made attempts and how to decide what form of aftercare is appropriate in each case. In the fifth chapter, an approach to brief treatment of patients who do not require hospital care is described in sufficient detail to serve as a therapist's practical 'manual'. Five case descriptions provided in Chapter 6 illustrate the use of this approach in clinical practice. Psychiatric inpatient care of attempted suicide patients is described in Chapter 7. Chapter 8 is devoted to the problem of deliberate self-injury, because this is often associated with special problems and may require other forms of treatment than those already described. The organization of services for attempted suicide patients is discussed in Chapter 9 and suggestions made as to how traditional services might be improved. The very important issue of how attempted suicide may be prevented is explored in Chapter 10, where results of recent treatment studies are also discussed. In the final chapter, the most important issues and needs in this field are summarized. There is a list of recommended texts at the end of the last chapter which should be useful for the reader who wishes to explore further the problem of attempted suicide and its management.

2

The problem of attempted suicide

In this chapter the background to the problem of attempted suicide will be discussed to help the reader understand the challenge that this phenomenon poses for the health service. First, the extent of the behaviour will be described and then there will be a summary of the type of people it involves. The problems facing those who make attempts will be dealt with more fully in the next chapter. Secondly, the methods used in attempts will be reviewed because they are very relevant to our understanding of the behaviour, particularly in terms of the dangers it entails. Aspects of attempted suicide that are of extreme importance are that it is often repeated and that some patients who make attempts subsequently kill themselves. Clearly, the clinician must be aware of when these are likely to occur. Thirdly, therefore, the repetition of attempted suicide, and the association between attempted suicide and completed suicide will be considered in some detail. Finally, the attitudes shown by people towards attempted suicide will be discussed. This is an important aspect of the problem because the behaviour tends to evoke strong reactions from those involved with people who make attempts, including relatives, friends, and members of clinical services, and these attitudes and those of the community at large may be important in determining both why so many people make attempts and what results from their acts.

THE SIZE OF THE PROBLEM

A massive increase in the numbers of people taking intentional overdoses or deliberately injuring themselves occurred during the 1960s and early 1970s. There was evidence of this phenomenon throughout Britain (Alderson 1974) and the Western world in general (Weissman 1974; Wexler *et al.* 1978). Reports of increasing rates of attempted suicide came from several cities in Britain, including Edinburgh (Aitken *et al.* 1969; Holding *et al.* 1977), Oxford (Evans 1967; Bancroft *et al.* 1975), Sheffield (Smith 1972), and Newcastle (Smith and Davison 1971).

In Oxford, for example, a substantial rise in the rates of deliberate self-poisoning and self-injury was reported by Evans (1967) for the period 1962–5. As shown in Fig. 1, the rates rose rapidly thereafter such that a four-fold increase in the incidence of attempted suicide was found for Oxford City during the 10 years until early 1973 (Bancroft *et al.* 1975). Subsequently, the rates continued to rise more slowly and appeared to have reached a peak in the later 1970s (Hawton *et al.* 1982*a*). This peak was also noted elsewhere (Holding *et al.* 1977; Gibbons *et al.* 1978*b*). On the basis of published rates, Diekstra (1985) estimated that the annual total number of suicide attempts in the European Economic Community in 1976 was approximately 1 400 000. Since that time there has been a decline in the extent of the problem, which has been most marked in females (Fig. 1). For example, in a comparative study of Oxford and Edinburgh, rates of referral to general hospital psychiatric services of patients following attempts decreased between 1976 and 1984 by 27 per cent for females in Oxford and 24 per cent for those in Edinburgh. The corresponding percentage reductions for men were 22 per cent and 14 per cent (Platt *et al.*, in preparation). The reduction in attempts by self-poisoning during the past few years appears to have been a general phenomenon throughout the United Kingdom (Brewer and Farmer 1985).

What explanations are there for the changes in attempted suicide rates over the past two decades? Major social changes might be one factor. They could include, for example, the increase in marital breakdown and unemployment. However, increasing unemployment occurred at the time when attempted suicide rates were declining. Furthermore, there is no evidence that marital problems have become less common recently; indeed, divorce rates continue to increase. Changes in fashion (i.e. attitudes to suicide behaviour) might be another explanation, but this is virtually immune to investigation. As discussed later in this chapter, self-poisoning is by far the most common method used in attempts. Therefore, one should particularly examine why changes in rates of self-poisoning have occurred. Evidence of a clear correlation between medical self-poisoning and the prescribing of psychotropic drugs has been presented by Forster and Frost (1985) for the period when

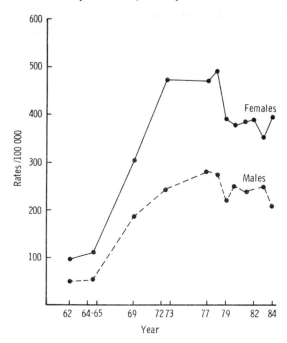

Fig. 1. Rates of general hospital admission for self-poisoning or self-injury among persons aged 15 and over in Oxford City, 1962–84.

deliberate self-poisoning was rapidly becoming more common. Furthermore, the recent decline in self-poisoning has paralleled a decline in prescribing of psychotropic drugs (Brewer and Farmer 1985). Such statistical associations do not, of course, demonstrate causal connections. However, the further evidence of the very high rates of psychotropic drug prescribing (including repeat prescription and multiple psychotropic drugs) for people who subsequently take overdoses (Hawton and Blackstock 1976; Prescott and Highley 1985) adds additional weight to a possible causal connection. While psychotropic drug prescribing could not explain all the recent changes in attempted suicide rates, we would argue that it is one important factor, especially when such drugs are prescribed inappropriately. This is discussed further in the chapter on prevention (p. 175).

The importance of attempted suicide for the health service is obvious, particularly when one considers that in many parts of

Britain deliberate self-poisoning has remained, in spite of the recent reduction in rates, the most common reason why women are admitted as emergencies to general hospitals, and the second most common reason (after ischaemic heart disease) for similar admissions of men. For many years the management of attempted suicide patients referred to hospital has posed considerable demands on medical and psychiatric services. This has resulted in productive efforts to improve clinical services. This book describes the results of such work.

Most research concerning the problem of deliberate self-poisoning and self-injury has been based on patients referred to general hospitals. It is clear that the phenomenon occurs more widely than this method of detection suggests. A survey of general practitioners in Edinburgh indicated that they might be seeing as many as 30 per cent more cases than those referred to hospital (Kennedy and Kreitman 1973). A more extensive epidemiological investigation in Canada took into account episodes of self-poisoning and self-injury which occurred in institutions, such as psychiatric hospitals, prisons, and nursing homes, and were not referred to hospitals, as well as cases treated out of hospital by family doctors (Whitehead *et al.* 1973). This survey indicated that the phenomenon is far more widespread than seems likely on the basis of findings for general hospital admissions. More than two-thirds of the total number of episodes identified would not have been detected in a survey confined to the general hospital.

Clearly, it is not only hospital-based medical and psychiatric services that face considerable demands in dealing with patients who have taken overdoses or injured themselves; the problem is one which also impinges to a marked degree on the work of general practitioners, social services, and many voluntary agencies.

THE CHARACTERISTICS OF PEOPLE ATTEMPTING SUICIDE

Age and sex

The age and sex distribution of people referred to hospital after deliberate self-poisoning and self-injury is illustrated in Fig. 2, which shows recent findings for Oxford City. It was clear from Fig. 1 that deliberate self-poisoning and self-injury are more common in females. The ratio of the number of females attempting suicide to the number of males is usually found to be in the range 1.5–2.1:1, although there has been a marked reduction in the sex ratio in recent years due to the relative decline in the rates among females (Platt *et al.*, in preparation).

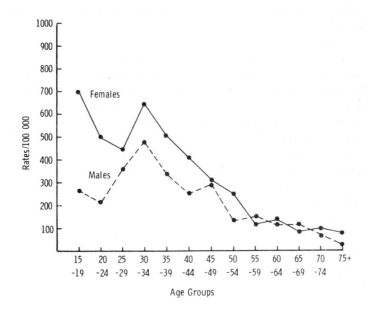

Fig. 2. Mean annual rates of attempted suicide among persons in Oxford City, 1980–84, by age and sex.

Figure 2 shows that the behaviour occurs most often among younger people. The highest rates for females are found in the age group 15–19. However, the rates in this group have declined recently, having been so high in the mid-1970's that 1 in a 100 girls of this age in the general population were referred to general hospitals each year following attempted suicide. The highest rates for males in Oxford are found in the age group 30–34 (Fig. 2) in which more than one out of every 200 may be referred to hospital after such acts during any one year. This peak for males is not found universally. In Edinburgh, for example, at present the peak rates for males are in the age group 20–25 years (Platt *et al.*, in preparation). In both sexes, the rates decline substantially in middle age and are extremely low after the age of 60.

As already noted, attempted suicide is not just confined to adults; it is a major problem in teenagers, in whom deliberate self-poisoning is especially common. Among younger adolescents during the mid to late 1970s there was not the same levelling off in incidence as occurred among the population in general. Thus, in the Oxford Region between 1974 and 1979 the rate of deliberate self-poisoning among persons aged 12–15 increased by 35 per cent (Hawton and Goldacre 1985). The preponderance of female attempters is more marked among adolescents than in adults. Thus, of the adolescents aged 15 and 16 who were admitted to general hospitals in the Oxford Region for deliberate self-poisoning between 1974 and 1979, more than 80 per cent were girls.

The preponderance of females among adolescent self-poisoners requires explanation. Three possibilities have been put forward (Hawton 1986). First, girls may mature and face problems of adulthood, such as broken relationships with boyfriends, earlier than boys. These are the problems which most commonly precipitate attempts by teenagers (p. 36). Secondly, self-poisoning may be a more acceptable coping strategy for girls than for boys. Thus, boys only seem to resort to suicidal behaviour in the face of extreme difficulties (Hawton *et al.* 1982*b*). Thirdly, boys may have better access to alternative outlets for dealing with distress, such as aggressive behaviour or alcohol abuse.

Under the age of 12 attempted suicide is relatively rare. Interestingly, according to reports from Australia and the USA, the usual sex ratio is reversed in child attempters (Kosky 1982; Rosenthal and Rosenthal 1984). Although there have been recent reports of attempts in children aged under 5 years (e.g. Rosenthal and Rosenthal 1984), these appear to represent isolated cases. However, it should be borne in mind that attempts by children are far more likely to go unrecognized than those by adults (Hawton 1986).

Why should attempted suicide become increasingly common after the age of 12 years? One important factor may be that the concept of death develops late in childhood, with full awareness of the implications of death not being gained until early adolescence (Piaget 1960; Koocher 1974). Possibly, serious impulses towards suicidal behaviour do not occur until the concept of death has developed. Other factors which have been suggested include the rarity of depression in children, their close integration within the family, and the necessity for a marked degree of cognitive maturation before a child can develop feelings such as despair and hopelessness (Shaffer and Fisher 1981).

Socioeconomic characteristics and place of residence

Rates of attempted suicide are inversely correlated with social class (Holding *et al.* 1977). In Oxford in 1980–82, for example, the rate in social class V was more than eight times that in social classes I and II, while in Edinburgh there was a twelve-fold difference (Platt *et al.*, in preparation). Presumably, this largely reflects the far greater prevalence in the lower socio-economic groups of the problems that commonly lead to suicide attempts (Chapter 3).

There is a very close association between unemployment and attempted suicide, especially in men. In view of the recent drastic increase in unemployment rates in the United Kingdom the nature of this association requires elucidation. This is discussed further in the next chapter (p. 31).

Relatively high rates of completed suicide have been found in Oxford and Cambridge University students (Carpenter 1959; Hawton *et al.* 1978b), but this has not been the case for their American counterparts at Yale and Harvard (Parrish 1957; Eisenberg 1980). The Oxbridge situation has led people to assume that high rates of attempted suicide will also be found among students. In fact the reverse was found in a study of Oxford University students (Hawton *et al.* 1978b). Rates of attempted suicide were much lower among students of both sexes during term-time than among other people of comparable age in Oxford City during the same period. The very different social class distribution of the students compared with the general population and the possibly unfashionable nature of attempted suicide among students might explain this finding. However, very similar types of problems were associated with attempts by students and those by young people in the general population in the Oxford study, the most common being the break-up of an important relationship.

The behaviour is more common in urban areas and also in areas of relative social deprivation and overcrowding. The highest rates of attempted suicide in Oxford City have been found in disadvantaged sections of council estates (Skrimshire 1976). High-rate areas outside the city include caravan sites and some council estates, particularly where there are poor amenities and other evidence of social disadvantage. High rates in Southampton were found in areas characterized by considerable residential mobility and the presence of hostels and cheap furnished accommodation (Gibbons *et al.* 1978*b*). In Edinburgh (Holding *et al.* 1977) and Bristol (Morgan *et al.* 1975*b*) the areas with the highest rates were also the most deprived, and those in Bristol were notable in addition for their overcrowding.

Marital status

The association between attempted suicide and marital status is by no means simple, but seems to vary with age and between the sexes. Thus, in Oxford, particularly high rates have been found for teenage wives, and single and divorced women aged 24–35 years, and in single men aged 30–40 years (Bancroft *et al.* 1975; Platt *et al.*, in preparation). The occurrence of attempted suicide in married subjects is far more common where the marital relationship has recently been disrupted through separation. In Edinburgh the highest rates for both sexes occur among the divorced (Holding *et al.* 1977; Platt *et al.*, in preparation).

THE METHODS USED

In the UK approximately nine out of ten cases of attempted suicide referred to general hospitals involve self-poisoning, the rest being self-injuries, or self-poisoning and self-injury combined. In describing in more detail the methods used, self-poisoning and self-injury can be considered separately.

Deliberate self-poisoning

Most overdoses involve prescribed drugs, with minor tranquillizers and sedatives being the most commonly used of these (see Fig. 3). This applies particularly to individuals in middle age. Non-opiate analgesics (e.g. aspirin and paracetamol) are now used more often than minor tranquillizers and sedatives, and have not usually been prescribed. They are involved considerably more often in the overdoses of younger persons, especially adolescents (Hawton and Goldacre 1982). During the 1970s the incidence of self-poisoning with paracetamol and paracetamol-containing substances increased. This has been a source of concern because liver damage can occur when paracetamol is taken in overdosage (Davidson and Eastham 1966).

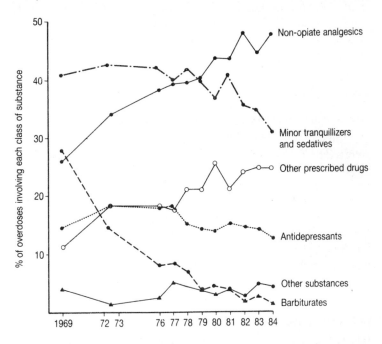

Fig. 3. Trends in substances used in self-poisoning in Oxford, 1969–84 (admissions only).

Self-poisoning with prescribed drugs partly seems to reflect how often such drugs are prescribed. Thus, barbiturate overdoses used to be common, but during the 1970s there was a steady fall in the numbers of such overdoses, in parallel with the reduction in prescribing of barbiturates. Similarly, there has been a recent decline in the numbers of minor tranquillizer overdoses (Fig. 3) at a time when there is much greater caution about the prescribing of these drugs.

As can be seen from Fig. 3, various other drugs and substances may be used in overdoses, although far less commonly than tranquillizers and sedatives and non-opiate analgesics. They include other psychotropic agents (e.g. antidepressants), a wide range of other prescribed drugs (e.g. anticonvulsants and antibiotics), and various substances which are not intended for ingestion (e.g. disinfectant). Where prescribed drugs are used for self-poisoning, very often these have been prescribed for the patient shortly before the overdose. This applies particularly to psychotropic agents (p. 40).

Despite the obvious dangers inherent in self-poisoning, the self-poisoners themselves are often unaware of the extent of toxicity of the substances consumed. This applies especially to overdoses of substances such as paracetamol (Gazzard *et al.* 1976). Physicians in Oxford were asked to rate a random series of patients' overdoses according to the outcome they would predict if the individuals involved had not received medical attention. They predicted certain or probable death in 7 per cent, little risk of death in 32 per cent, and certain survival in 61 per cent. Although most overdoses were judged to be relatively 'safe', the chance nature of the behaviour in terms of life and death is very clear. Indeed risk-taking seems to be an important integral aspect of some cases of self-poisoning. When the same series of patients were asked about suicidal intent at the time of their overdoses, a third of them said they did not mind whether they lived or died (Bancroft *et al.* 1979).

Deliberate self-injury

The most common form of deliberate self-injury involves self-cutting, particularly of the wrists and arms, although other parts of the body are sometimes cut. Wrist-cutting, which is predominantly a behaviour of younger patients, is often repeated and in many cases appears to be a different phenomenon in psychopathological terms from self-poisoning. The act of cutting is usually carried out in a state of detachment and may be motivated by a need to alleviate intolerable tension.

In the UK, other forms of self-injury—such as shooting, attempted drowning, and jumping from heights—tend to involve older people and are nearly always associated with serious suicidal intent. In other words, many of those who survive these acts had hoped that they would die. Such acts, especially shooting, are much more common in the USA. Shooting usually results in death. Suicide rates in the USA rose between 1953 and 1973, but entirely because of an increase in rates of suicide by means of firearms from 4.9 to 7.1 per 100 000 population per year (Boyd 1983). However, a recent study of survivors of self-inflicted firearm injuries suggested that these include some individuals with similar characteristics of completed suicides (i.e. they were 'failed suicides'), and some who were much more like attempters. In this latter group the shooting was impulsive and there was ambivalence about dying (Peterson *et al.* 1985). Thus, it is possible that, if in a different environment in which firearms were not readily available, some individuals who die from shooting might choose a less dangerous method and hence survive their attempts. This worrying suggestion adds further fuel to the arguments in favour of limiting firearm sales in the USA.

Occasionally, patients are admitted to hospital having mutilated themselves in some way. Such patients are usually suffering from serious psychiatric disorder. These and other forms of self-injury are discussed more fully in Chapter 8.

Use of alcohol

Severe intoxication with alcohol may in some cases be regarded as deliberate self-poisoning, and as such akin to taking an overdose of tablets. Very often alcohol is also associated with attempted suicide. Thus, in Oxford in 1984, alcohol was consumed during the act in approximately 25 per cent of attempts, and in more of those made by men than by women. In addition, alcohol is often consumed shortly before an attempt. Among self-poisoners in Oxford in 1984, approximately half the men and almost a third of the women admitted to having been drinking during the 6 hours before their overdoses. Similar findings have been noted elsewhere, such as Bristol (Morgan *et al.* 1975*a*), although in Edinburgh a far higher proportion of both male and female self-poisoners report drinking beforehand (Holding *et al.* 1977; Platt *et al.*, in preparation). This may reflect the greater prevalence of alcohol-related problems in Scotland.

REPETITION OF ATTEMPTED SUICIDE

A major problem of self-poisoning and self-injury is that many people repeat the behaviour. The proportion of patients re-referred within a year to the same general hospital to which they were admitted for previous attempts is between 12 and 25 per cent (Morgan *et al.* 1976; Bancroft and Marsack 1977; Kreitman 1977). This does not take account of those who repeat but are not referred to hospital, those who repeat and are referred elsewhere, and those who repeat attempts and die without being admitted to hospital.

Repeats are most likely to occur during the 3 months after a previous episode (Bancroft and Marsack 1977). Some patients undertake more than one repeat. Bancroft and Marsack suggested that there are three types of repeaters: the *chronic repeater* who tends to move from one crisis to another, with self-poisoning or self-injury as an habitual method of coping (this problem is considered further below); the person who has *several repeats within a few months*, perhaps extending over a relatively prolonged period of stress, such as a marital conflict, but who then stops for quite a long while; and the '*one-off person*' who takes an overdose at a time of severe crisis and who may occasionally repeat.

The identification of patients most likely to repeat is obviously very important and is discussed in detail in Chapter 4. Factors found to characterize such patients are problems in the use of alcohol, personality disorder, a history of previous inpatient or outpatient psychiatric treatment, previous attempts resulting in admission to hospital, and not living with relatives (Buglass and Horton 1974).

The chronic repeater

People who repeatedly make attempts pose very difficult problems for medical and psychiatric services in the general hospital. Apart from expenditure of medical time and resources, the recurrence of self-poisoning or self-injury may antagonize the staff involved in the care of such patients, who are likely to feel that their therapeutic efforts have been wasted. At the same time such patients have an increased risk of suicide, and usually experience serious personality and social problems.

Chronic repeaters represent a relatively small proportion of the total population of attempted suicide patients referred to general hospitals, but they are usually conspicuous and well known to staff because of the nature of their behaviour. In a two-year follow-up study of a cohort of 690 attempters in Oxford, Bancroft and Marsack (1977) found that 7 per cent made two repeats or more, 17 (2.5 per cent) repeated three or more times and eight (1 per cent) repeated five times or more. The proportion of chronic repeaters would have been underestimated slightly because the findings were based only on referrals in the Oxford area; patients who repeated elsewhere would not have been detected. Very similar results were obtained in a one- to two-year follow-up study in Bristol (Morgan *et al.* 1976). A history of four or more previous attempts was found in 18.8 per cent of attempters referred to a Toronto hospital (Barnes 1979).

As would be expected, Barnes (1979) found a positive association between the number of attempts a person makes and the chances of their having received psychiatric treatment or having been admitted to a psychiatric hospital. All the patients in her sample with a history of four or more attempts had received inpatient treatment, and virtually all had received other forms of psychiatric care. In the USA many such patients would, because of their repeat attempts and associated characteristics, receive a DSM III diagnosis of 'borderline personality' (p. 35).

Repetition of attempted suicide increases the chances that an individual will subsequently die from suicide. Among a series of suicides, Ovenstone and Kreitman (1974) identified a subgroup of individuals who had made multiple previous attempts. They were also characterized by persistent interpersonal and social problems complicated by alcoholism or drug addiction. When an attempt by a chronic repeater appears to have involved greater suicidal intent than previous episodes this may be an indication of even greater risk of eventual suicide (Pierce 1981).

The reasons why individuals repeatedly take overdoses or inflict self-injuries are often unclear. This makes the task of helping such patients even more difficult. Some patients, lacking sufficient or appropriate coping resources to surmount their difficulties, may repeat to avoid facing up to their problems. Others may take overdoses or cut themselves to deal with intolerable feelings of tension. A few patients appear to obtain some sort of excitement from the risk-taking that is entailed. Finally, patients who repeat several times may feel they need the attention of hospital staff that each episode brings. One such patient was a young man who took many overdoses and claimed to take others where supporting evidence from blood samples was lacking. Eventually, he admitted to a therapist that he wished to gain repeated hospital admissions to get care and physical attention from female nursing staff. He had never been able to form relationships with the opposite sex outside hospital. The assessment and treatment of the chronic repeater will be discussed later (pp. 79 and 106).

THE RELATIONSHIP BETWEEN ATTEMPTED SUICIDE AND SUICIDE

Attempted suicide and completed suicide can be considered largely as separate phenomena but with an important area of overlap. It is surprising that some authors, particularly in the USA, treat all suicidal behaviours as a single entity. This is clearly inappropriate for several reasons. First, rates of suicide and attempted suicide have changed independently over recent years. The official suicide rates both for men and for women in Britain fell substantially between 1962 and 1976 (Office of Health Economics 1981). During this time, as has already been noted, the rates for non-fatal deliberate self-poisoning and self-injury were rapidly increasing. Subsequently, there was some parallel increase in rates of both suicide and attempted suicide during the late 1970s, followed in the early 1980s by a considerable decline in rates of attempted suicide (p. 8), but not of suicide. Secondly, there are marked differences between the characteristics of those who engage in the two forms of behaviour. Thus, for example, suicide becomes more common with increasing age, when it more commonly involves men; whereas, as already discussed, attempted suicide is far more common among young people, when it more commonly involves women. In addition, whereas most people who kill themselves are suffering from psychiatric disorders (Barraclough *et al.* 1974), this applies only to a minority of those who make attempts (p. 34). Third, suicide often entails violent means, such as hanging and shooting, whereas self-poisoning is the usual method of attempted suicide.

The ratio of the rate of attempted suicide to the rate of suicide was 10.8:1 in Edinburgh in 1970 (Ovenstone 1973). However, it is more revealing to look at the ratios according to sex and age. The ratio for women (14.2:1) was twice that of the ratio for men (7.7:1). This was partly because of the sex difference for attempted suicide and partly because of the sex difference for suicide. In adults under 34 years of age, attempted suicide was more than 30 times as common as suicide, whereas in those over 55 years of age attempted suicide was only about three times more common than suicide.

Table 1

Suicide following attempted suicide

	Numbers of attempted suicide patients	Followup (years)	Suicides (%)
Kessel and McCulloch (1966)	511	1	1.6
Buglass and Horton (1974)	2809	1	0.8
Hawton and Fagg (in preparation)	1626	1	1.0
Greer and Bagley (1971)	204	1½	2.0
Stengel and Cook (1958)	210	2–5	1.4
Buglass and McCulloch (1970)	511	3	3.3
Hawton and Fagg (in preparation)	1335	8	2.8

Having considered the important differences between attempted suicide and completed suicide, the association between the two phenomena must now be emphasized. First, a small but very important proportion of patients who make attempts go on to kill themselves. Several studies have been conducted in the UK to determine the size of this group (Table 1). Approximately 1 per cent of attempters will die by suicide during the year following their attempts, which is about one-hundred times the annual risk of suicide in the general population. The first year, especially the first six months (Hawton and Fagg, in preparation), is the period of greatest risk, but as can be seen from the table, the risk of suicide continues to be high several years after an attempt. Secondly, a substantial proportion of individuals in the general population who kill themselves have made previous attempts. In a study of suicides in Edinburgh (Ovenstone and Kreitman 1974), it was found that 47 per cent had a history of previous attempts. When this 'overlap' group was compared, first, with attempted suicide patients and, secondly, with another group of suicides with no history of attempts, it appeared that this group more closely resembled the other suicide group than the attempted suicide patients, especially in terms of sex and age. However, the overlap group was distinguished from both the other groups by its high content of individuals with serious personality difficulties ('sociopathy'), drug addiction, alcoholism, unemployment, and criminal behaviour.

In summary, there are considerable group differences between individuals who make attempts and those who kill themselves. However, there is an important overlap group. In the management of attempted suicide, special care must be given to the detection and treatment of those at risk of subsequent suicide. This will be discussed more fully in subsequent chapters (pp. 66 and 145).

ATTITUDES TOWARDS ATTEMPTED SUICIDE

An important, but often neglected aspect of the problem of attempted suicide concerns the attitudes shown by people towards the behaviour. The attitudes of those who take medical or psychiatric responsibility for patients who have made attempts are likely to influence the sort of care patients receive. The attitudes of relatives and friends, on whom the behaviour is liable to impinge most severely, will determine their response to the behaviour. In addition, knowledge of attitudes towards attempted suicide among the community in general may help us understand more about why the behaviour is so common and also provide clues for prevention.

Clearly, the behaviour is likely to evoke intense and extreme attitudes. These will vary according to how it is understood both in terms of the problems that appear to have precipitated it and the apparent intentions of the person involved. This was demonstrated in a study of general hospital doctors' and nurses' attitudes to self-poisoning (Ramon *et al.* 1975). Doctors in particular differentiated clearly between patients whom they thought had been trying to kill themselves and those to whom they attributed other motives, especially where these were of a manipulative nature. They showed relatively accepting attitudes towards the first type of patient, but showed unsympathetic attitudes towards the latter type. Such attitudes are perhaps understandable in view of the pressures under which junior medical staff have to work. Self-induced disorder is likely to be seen as an unwelcome extra load, particularly where this has occurred in response to problems of living rather than illness. Nevertheless, their attitudes may have important implications for the management of patients (pp. 59 and 93).

Similar differences in attitudes to overdose patients according to the perceived motivation were found by Hawton *et al.* (1981*b*) in a study of psychiatrists, using the same methodology as in Ramon's study. However, the psychiatrists differed from the physicians in the earlier study in that their attitudes were generally more sympathetic and they expressed greater willingness to help the patients. These findings probably reflect the different roles of physicians and psychiatrists in the management of overdose patients, and the differing extents to which such patients are viewed by the two groups of doctors as being relevant to their work.

Surprisingly little attention has been paid to the ways in which people close to attempters interpret and react to the behaviour, especially as the most common problems preceding overdoses are difficulties in relationships with either partners (p. 29) or parents (p. 36), and the reactions of such people usually have important implications for both aftercare and outcome. James and Hawton (1985) addressed this topic by comparing the reasons chosen by the closest relatives or friends ('significant-others') of 34 self-poisoners and by the self-poisoners themselves, to explain the overdoses, and by examining the attitudes of the significant-others to the overdoses. While 41 per cent of the self-poisoners claimed suicidal intent as a reason for the overdoses, only one significant-other saw this as being a reason. The significant-others were more likely to attribute manipulative reasons, commonly viewing the overdoses as directed at themselves. However, the two groups tended to agree that the overdoses were often a means of alleviating distress. The significant-others also frequently reported a mixture of emotional reactions to the overdoses. Thus, as well as evoking sympathy, the overdoses often caused the significant-others to feel considerable guilt and anger. Contrary both to expectation and to the findings of the studies of hospital staff and psychiatrists discussed above, the amount of sympathy and guilt expressed by the significant-others bore no relation to the self-poisoners' degree of suicidal intent, as measured by the Beck Suicidal Intent Scale (Beck *et al.* 1974*a*). There was, however, a weak positive association between the amount of anger the significant-others reported and the apparent degree of suicidal intent. The clinical implications of these findings are that friends and relatives may find it easier to offer support to self-poisoners following their overdoses if clinicians first encourage expression of the mixed feelings evoked by the behaviour, explaining that such feelings are understandable, and if the differences in explanations for the overdoses are explored in subsequent therapy (p. 104).

There is also little objective evidence about the attitudes of the general population to suicidal behaviour, although as many as half (Sale *et al.* 1975), and possibly more (Ginsburg 1971), have had personal experience of it. However, it appears that more sympathetic attitudes are associated with suicidal behaviour of high suicidal intent, and unsympathetic attitudes with behaviour that is seen as manipulative (Sale *et al.* 1975). Less favourable attitudes are shown by those who have personal experience of attempted suicide in a friend or relative (Sale *et al.* 1975), although not surprisingly the converse was found for psychiatric patients who had themselves taken overdoses in the past (Hawton *et al.* 1978*a*). An important finding that has emerged from studying attitudes of patients and those of the general population is that both suicide and attempted suicide often appear to be regarded as phenomena that happen to a person, rather than events the person intentionally brings about (Ginsburg 1971; Bancroft *et al.* 1979).

CONCLUSIONS

The main aim of this chapter has been to demonstrate the importance of the problem of attempted suicide for all who are involved in clinical medicine, psychiatry, or social work, whether they be based in hospitals or in the community. During the 1960s and 1970s attempted suicide emerged as one of the major challenges facing health and social services. Despite a substantial decrease in the extent of this behaviour in the early 1980s, attempted suicide remains a significant health care problem. This is partly because of the sheer size of the problem in terms of numbers of individuals it involves, but also because it reflects considerable personal and social distress, and in some cases leads to actual suicide. Attempted suicide tends to evoke strong reactions from people, including doctors and nurses on medical wards, relatives and friends, and also the general public. Such reactions have important implications for the hospital care and aftercare of patients. The next chapter provides an account of the antecedents and consequences of attempted suicide, including the problems faced by people who make attempts, the explanations they give for their actions, and the changes that may occur as a result of their behaviour.

3

The circumstances surrounding attempted suicide

The provision of appropriate help for people who take overdoses or deliberately injure themselves will depend to a large extent on having a thorough understanding of the circumstances in which attempts occur. These include: (a) the problems that are faced by such people; (b) the extent to which they have contacted helping agencies before attempts and the results of such contacts; (c) the motivational aspects of the behaviour, including how long people think about attempts beforehand, and the explanations they and other people give for them; and (d) the consequences of attempts. In this chapter these important factors will be considered particularly with respect to self-poisoning (self-injury will be dealt with in more detail in Chapter 8).

PROBLEMS

An obvious first step in trying to understand attempted suicide is to look closely at the types of problems facing patients who make attempts. For practical purposes these can be divided into problems which occur shortly beforehand, and which have often acted as precipitants, and longer-term or chronic problems in the context of which acute problems have arisen. In addition, the important role of psychiatric disorder in some cases of attempted suicide must be considered. Finally, account needs to be taken of the special problems faced by many adolescent attempters.

Acute problems

Most instances of self-poisoning or self-injury are preceded by stressful events. In a study in New Haven, Connecticut, suicide attempters were found to have experienced a greater number of life events (mean 3.3) in the 6 months preceding attempts than either well-matched depressed patients (mean 2.1) before the onset of their symptoms, or similarly matched subjects from the general population (mean 0.8) before their interviews (Paykel *et al.* 1975). Thus, the attempted suicide patients had on average experienced four times as many life events as their general population controls. In particular they more often reported the following events: serious argument with the spouse; having a new person in the home; serious illness of a family member; serious personal physical illness; and having to appear in court for an offence. The suicide attempters were especially likely to have been involved recently in a major row. The occurrence of life events increased to a peak during the month preceding the attempt and was most marked in the week beforehand.

The results of this American study have been borne out to a substantial degree by research in this country. A detailed investigation was carried out in Oxford of the events occurring during the week before attempts and those anticipated as likely to occur in the near future (Bancroft *et al.* 1977). One-hundred-and-thirty randomly selected patients were included in the study. The term 'event' was used to describe an episode which either involved or was relevant to the patient, was not part of a normal day's routine (such as going to work), and which had a recognizable end. Events involving a key person far exceeded in incidence both events which did not involve key persons and impending events.

Events involving a relationship with a key person
Here 'key person' refers to a member of the individual's extended or nuclear family, or boyfriend or girlfriend. The event that stood out in this respect from all others was a 'quarrel' which had occurred within a week of the attempt for 48 per cent of the patients. Most of these quarrels occurred during the 2 days before the attempt and they occurred more often for women than men. An example was a woman whose husband spent six evenings a week out drinking with friends. When one morning she finally confronted him with how neglected she felt and asked him to take her out with him, he flew into a rage and told her to mind her own business. She took an overdose shortly before he got home from work that evening.

In addition, several patients had separated from their partners, some had experienced behaviour of a partner or relative which was upsetting or rejecting, and in a few cases infidelity had occurred.

Events not involving a key person

These were much less common. Apart from a few cases where the events had involved work in some way (e.g. being sacked), the rest were very diverse. An example was a woman who took an overdose shortly after being raped by two men.

Impending events

These were also relatively infrequent. Most involved events which were expected to occur more than a week ahead. They included, for example, court cases, school examinations, and a near relative about to undergo surgery.

Chronic problems

In the same study (Bancroft *et al.* 1977), 'chronic problems' were arbitrarily defined as difficulties which had existed for more than 1 week preceding the attempts. The most common chronic problems are summarized in Table 2 and will now be considered in more detail, both with regard to the original investigation and to subsequent findings.

Table 2

Types of chronic problems experienced by 130 suicide attempters. Results are given as percentages of those subjects for whom each problem was applicable

Problems	Females (n=91)	Males (n=39)	Both (n=130)
Marital	68	83	72
Boyfriend/girlfriend	70.5	77	72
Sexual	14	15	15
Children	26	17	26
Financial	16	26	19
Work	16	54	28
Accident/operation	19	2.5	14
Alcohol	9	9	9

Marital and other relationship problems

More than two-thirds of those who were married had marital problems. Half the married men had been involved in extramarital relationships during the preceding year. This also applied to a small minority of women. Over a quarter of the men and one in eight of the women reported recent infidelity on the part of their spouses. Some of those with marital problems had separated shortly before their attempts. A similar proportion of those who were unmarried were having difficulties in their relationships with boyfriends or girlfriends.

The most common constellation of acute and chronic problems was a very recent quarrel or separation in the context of longer-term marital problems or difficulties with a boyfriend or girlfriend.

Sexual problems

The sexual problems noted in Table 2 were often closely associated with general difficulties in the relationship with the partner. It has been suggested that problems associated with homosexuality may cause homosexuals to be at particular risk of attempted suicide (Saghir and Robins 1973; Bell and Weinberg 1978). In an investigation of this potential association Catalan (1983) failed to confirm this suggestion. Recent changes in attitudes towards homosexuality may explain the difference between the findings of his investigation and earlier studies. The most common problem faced by the homosexuals in Catalan's study was, just as in attempts by heterosexuals, the threatened or actual break-up of a relationship. However, at least half of the homosexuals who had attempted suicide appeared to have problems coping with their sexual orientation.

Problems with children

Approximately a quarter of the patients had problems with their children. Recently, further information has come to light concerning the association between problems with children and attempted suicide. Roberts and Hawton (1980) found that parents who abuse or neglect their children, and those regarded as at special risk of doing so, have very high rates of attempted suicide. In an investigation of 114 families where the children had been abused or neglected, or were regarded at risk of so being, 29 per cent contained at least one parent who had taken an overdose or injured themselves. There did not appear to be a clear time relationship between the suicidal behaviour and abuse, although in two cases the parents had been trying to kill both themselves and the children. In only a few cases the attempt appeared to be a warning that the parents could not cope with their children. More commonly, the occurrence of both attempts and abuse appeared to result from marital problems and personality difficulties. A history of psychiatric disorder and of marital breakdown was more common among child-abuse parents who had made attempts than among those who had not.

One example from this study was a young army wife, who, by the age of 20, had borne four live children and one stillborn infant. She took an overdose 2 months after the birth of her fourth child, who was then referred to a children's hospital because of serious neglect. The mother appeared to be exhausted and disillusioned by premature marriage and motherhood. She and her husband admitted being uninterested in the children. Her overdose seemed to be an attempt to escape from the domestic situation. She finally deserted the family, taking with her only one of her children.

In a further investigation of the association between child abuse and parental attempted suicide, Hawton *et al.* (1985) studied mothers, with children aged five or under, who took overdoses, in order to determine how common child abuse, neglect, and risk of abuse were in such families, both before the overdoses and subsequently. Using a similar method of investigation for each group, a comparison was first made between the children of mothers who attempted suicide and those of mothers in the general population, and those of mothers at risk of depression. While no cases of abuse, neglect, or risk of abuse were found in the general population group and only 4.7 per cent in the at risk for depression group, 15.8 per cent were found among the attempted suicide mothers. When a more extensive method of identification of child care problems was applied to the attempted suicide mothers, overall 29 per cent had children who had been abused or neglected (6.1 per cent), or were officially regarded as 'at risk'. While most of these problem families had been identified before the attempts, some were only identified during the following year. These findings have demonstrated the importance, when assessing a mother who has taken an overdose, of not focusing exclusively on the woman (and her partner), but also of considering the relationship with her children and notifying her family doctor if there is any cause for concern.

It is also known that suicide attempters, especially young attempters, have often themselves been abused as children (McCulloch and Philip 1972; Green 1978). Parental suicidal behaviour, child abuse and neglect, and suicidal acts in adolescence and adulthood may therefore represent a continuing cycle of internally and externally directed aggression within families.

Work problems and unemployment

Employment problems were common among male attempters in the Oxford study (Table 2). In many cases the men were unemployed. Since the time of that study, and in the light of the massive increase in unemployment rates that occurred in the United Kingdom during the late 1970s and early 1980s, the association between unemployment and attempted suicide has been the subject of considerable investigation, notably in Edinburgh and Oxford.

Among men there is a clear association between unemployment and attempted suicide. For example, in Edinburgh between 1968 and 1982 the incidence of attempted suicide in men was nearly always more than 10 times higher in the unemployed than among the employed (Platt and Kreitman 1984), and in Oxford between 1979 and 1982 the incidence was 12 to 15 times higher in unemployed men (Hawton and Rose 1986). During the recession of the late 1970s and early 1980s the proportions of male attempters who were unemployed rose each year in parallel with the increasing unemployment rate. For example, in Oxford between 1979 and 1982, male unemployment increased from 4.8 to 9.9 per cent while the proportion of male attempters who were unemployed rose from 41 to 66 per cent. However, there were discrepancies between different centres in terms of whether overall attempted suicide rates in men increased with rising unemployment. This appears to have been the case in Edinburgh between 1968 and 1982, but not in either Oxford, in the South of England, between 1979 and 1983, or Hartlepool, in the North, between 1974 and 1983 (Furness *et al.* 1985). Such apparently conflicting findings may reflect geographical differences in terms of the personal impact of unemployment.

Risk of attempted suicide also increases dramatically the longer a man is unemployed. In Oxford in 1982, for example, the risk among men unemployed up to 1 year was just over eight times that of the employed, whereas in men unemployed more than a year the risk was 26 times that of the employed. There was also a suggestion from the Edinburgh study of elevated risk during the four weeks following loss of a job by comparison with the subsequent 21 weeks of unemployment.

The interpretation of these findings is not straightforward and has given rise to much debate (Shapiro and Perry 1984; Platt and Kreitman 1985*a*; Smith 1985*b*; Hawton and Rose 1986). It seems unlikely, for example, that unemployment itself is a direct cause of attempts, except very occasionally. However, there is good evidence that unemployment causes deterioration in mental health (Smith 1985*a*), and this might be one reason for the association between attempted suicide and unemployment. Equally feasible are other explanations, including that people with poorer mental health (and therefore greater risk of making attempts) are more likely to become unemployed, or that both unemployment and attempted suicide are caused by other factors, such as poverty or alcohol problems.

A single explanation is unlikely to account for the entire association and probably all of those mentioned above are relevant to some degree. There may also be differences in the psychological impact of unemployment in different age groups, with possibly less impact in the young, among whom unemployment is a common expectation, and greater impact in older persons because of a long history of expectation of employment (Hawton and Rose 1986). The impact of unemployment on the individual may also differ between areas of high and those of low unemployment, possibly being greater in the latter (Platt and Kreitman 1985*b*). Further elucidation of this phenomenon by carefully designed research studies is clearly required. However, at present one has to rely largely on the common clinical experience that many of the domestic, financial, social, and psychological problems faced by some men who make attempts appear either to be caused or aggravated by unemployment.

Little is known about how attempted suicide relates to unemployment among women. This is probably because of the difficulties inherent in defining female employment status. However, preliminary work suggests that there is an increased risk of attempted suicide among unemployed women which is at least as great as that in unemployed men, and that there is a similar rise in risk with duration of unemployment (Hawton *et al.* in preparation).

Physical health

There is a greater incidence of poor physical health and recent general hospital admissions among attempters than would be expected. In the Oxford study, 22.5 per cent of men and 34 per cent of women had been admitted to a general hospital for reasons other than suicide attempts during the year preceding their attempts. As can be seen in Table 2, almost one in five of the women had recently had accidents or undergone surgery.

Although the reasons for medical admissions are diverse, an association has been demonstrated between epilepsy and attempted suicide (Mackay 1979; Hawton *et al.* 1980). Patients with epilepsy are between five and seven times more commonly represented among the attempted suicide population than would be expected on the basis of general population rates of epilepsy. Males with epilepsy are particularly over-represented. The patients with epilepsy make more repeat attempts than attempters in general and appear to be a particularly disturbed group, which is reflected in the large number who have received previous psychiatric treatment.

Considerable controversy has surrounded the question of whether suicide attempts in women are more likely during a particular phase of the menstrual cycle. Thus, while some studies have shown an increased risk of attempts in either the premenstrual or menstrual phases (Dalton 1959; Trautman 1961; Tonks *et al.* 1968), others have failed to demonstrate any such association (Buckle *et al.* 1965; Birtchnell and Floyd 1974, 1975). There are major methodological difficulties in studying this problem, the variability in length of the menstrual cycle being one. While the known increased incidence of psychological disturbances during the premenstrual phase and the association between complaints of premenstrual symptoms and psychiatric disorder (Clare 1983) would make any association between suicide attempts and the premenstrual phase understandable, at present this association has not been conclusively proven.

Problems with alcohol

In the Oxford study, the proportion (9 per cent) of the male subjects thought to have problems with alcohol (Table 2) was far lower than equivalent figures at the time from elsewhere. In

Edinburgh, for example, 48 per cent of male attempters were found
to have alcohol problems (Holding *et al.* 1977), and in Bristol a
figure of 36 per cent was obtained (Morgan *et al.* 1975a). These
differences probably reflected the use of different criteria for the
diagnosis of alcohol problems rather than actual regional differences.
Thus, when similar criteria were used in each centre, in 1983–4
alcoholism was diagnosed in just over 14 per cent of male
attempters and 5 per cent of female attempters in Edinburgh, and in
just over 22 per cent of male attempters and 4 per cent of female
attempters in Oxford (Platt *et al.*, in preparation).

In spite of the differences in the specific proportions of attempters
who are diagnosed in different centres as being alcoholic, there is
clearly a very marked association between attempted suicide and
alcoholism, especially in men. This may relate largely to the effects
of alcohol abuse on social adjustment, and mental and physical
health. However, the disinhibiting effects of alcohol when suicidal
urges are experienced may be another factor. Thus, it has already
been noted that alcohol is often consumed before attempts by both
sexes (p. 17).

Other problems

The more common problems faced by suicide attempters, apart
from psychiatric disorders, have now been considered. However, a
wide variety of other problems are encountered when working with
such patients. It is also noteworthy that although many attempted
suicide patients have experienced some form of recent loss, usually
in the form of a separation, bereavement does not appear to be a
frequent event preceding attempts. This is in contrast to the finding
for completed suicide where recent death of a parent or spouse is
relatively common (Sainsbury 1973). Finally, suicidal behaviour is
also associated with drug addiction, although relatively small
proportions of suicide attempters are drug addicts (almost 7 per
cent of male attempters and 3 per cent of female attempters in
Oxford during 1983–4).

Psychiatric disorder

The types of psychiatric symptoms and disorders experienced by
suicide attempters were investigated by Newson-Smith and Hirsch
(1979a) in a study of a series of patients who had taken overdoses.

The patients were assessed using the Present State Examination (Wing *et al.* 1974), which provides a systematic method of identifying psychiatric symptoms and diagnosing psychiatric illness. The symptoms identified as present most often during the 4 weeks before the overdoses were as follows: feelings of nervous tension (75 per cent), depressed mood (75 per cent), hopelessness (61 per cent), irritability (55 per cent), tension pains (49 per cent), worrying (45 per cent), and poor concentration (43 per cent).

Although psychiatric symptoms were common, the proportion of patients having 'definite' psychiatric disorder was only 31 per cent. In addition, a further 29 per cent of patients were in the borderline or 'threshold' category. All but one patient in these two groups were diagnosed as suffering from depressive disorders. In a similar study of self-poisoning patients, Urwin and Gibbons (1979) found that 30 per cent had definite disorders and 42 per cent were in the borderline group. Again most were suffering from depression, but there were also patients suffering from alcoholism, anxiety disorders, and schizophrenia. A quarter of the men and just over one in ten of the women were classified as having personality disorders. In the DSM III diagnostic system which is used in the USA, such patients would often be labelled, on the basis of DSM III, as having 'borderline personalities'. This diagnosic category includes people who show instability in a variety of areas, including interpersonal behaviours, mood, and self-image. Both categories, personality disorder, and borderline personality disorder, are too wide to be of much use, especially in planning management.

The patients in the first study (Newson-Smith and Hirsch 1979a) were interviewed again after 1 week and also 3 months later. After 1 week, 24 per cent of patients were in the definite illness category and 16 per cent were in the borderline group. At the 3 month interviews only 8 per cent were found to be in the definite illness category and 14 per cent in the borderline group.

Thus, although many patients who take overdoses have recently experienced psychiatric symptoms which in a sizeable proportion of cases indicate psychiatric disorder, for most of these patients the disorders are mild and mostly take the form of depression. In addition, the disorders in most cases are relatively transient. It appears that they are usually secondary to the types of difficulty in the patients' lives that were described earlier in this chapter. Nevertheless, it is important to note that a small proportion of attempted suicide patients, perhaps between 5 and 8 per cent, are suffering from severe psychiatric illnesses, which include psychotic depression and schizophrenia (Morgan *et al.* 1975*a*), and a further subgroup are dependent on alcohol (p. 33). Apart from needing psychiatric treatment, this group of patients contains those most likely to be at risk for subsequent suicide. In a study of a series of 100 individuals who had killed themselves, 70 per cent were thought to have been suffering from depression, 15 per cent from alcoholism, 3 per cent from schizophrenia, and 5 per cent from other conditions (Barraclough *et al.* 1974). The risk of eventual suicide in all patients who have serious depressive conditions has been estimated as being between 14 per cent (Robins *et al.* 1959) and 16 per cent (Pitts and Winokur 1964).

The problems faced by adolescents who take overdoses

It was noted in Chapter 2 that attempted suicide is common in young people and that adolescents, especially girls, form a sizeable proportion of the patients admitted to hospital after self-poisoning or self-injury. As might be expected, the problems facing such adolescents usually differ from those of their adult counterparts (Table 3). However, the most common general type of problem is similar, namely a recent row in the setting of a difficult relationship. The most common problem identified among a series of 50 adolescents (including 45 girls) aged 13–18 who had taken overdoses was in their relationships with their parents (Hawton *et al.* 1982*b*). Three-quarters had difficulties with either or both parents. The adolescents complained particularly about their inability to discuss problems with their parents, especially their fathers. Some overdoses were precipitated by a row with a parent.

The extent of disturbance in the adolescents' family backgrounds was further reflected in the findings that 36 per cent were living with only one parent, and 12 per cent with neither parent. In addition, 12 per cent had been 'in care' with social services at some time. These figures are all far higher than those for adolescents in general, and are consistent with findings of other studies in the United Kingdom (White 1974; Walker 1980) and from elsewhere in Europe (Bergstrand and Otto 1962; Choquet *et al.* 1980), the USA (Jacobs 1971; Rohn *et al.* 1977), and Canada (Garfinkel and

Table 3

Current problems identified for 50 adolescent self-poisoners

Problem area	% of subjects for whom each problem was applicable
Parents	76
School/work	58
Boy/girlfriend	52
Social isolation	28
Sibling(s)	22
Physical health	22
Psychiatric symptoms	20
Sexual	16
Relationship with peers	14
Alcohol	14
Physical illness of family member	14

Golombek 1983), all of which have demonstrated a high frequency of broken homes among adolescent suicide attempters.

More than half the adolescents in this study had problems at school, including both with their school work and in their relationships with teachers. Employment difficulties, including unemployment, were common among those who had left school. Half the adolescents had difficulties in their relationships with a boyfriend or girlfriend. A recent row or break in such a relationship was the most common precipitant of an overdose. Several adolescents had poor relationships with their peers. These difficulties most commonly took the form of social isolation due to lack of friends.

As in adults, there was common evidence of poor physical health. Thus, not only were recent general hospital admissions common, but almost a third of the adolescents reported having a physical disorder at the time of their overdoses. Although these disorders were not usually disabling, they were sometimes chronic (e.g. asthma, dysmenorrhoea) and seemed in some cases to have contributed to the overdoses in the sense of undermining ability to cope with other stresses.

Frank psychiatric disorder was rare although almost a quarter had seen a psychiatrist at some time. However, a small group of the adolescents appeared to be developing considerable personality difficulties, and some had moderately severe depressive symptoms although these were usually transient.

It was possible to classify the adolescents into three subgroups, which were distinguished not only according to family background and problems identified at the time of the overdoses but also in terms of subsequent outcome (Hawton *et al.* 1982*c*). The three subgroups were identified as follows.

Group I: 'Acute', which included subjects whose problems had persisted for less than 1 month. One in five of the adolescents were in this group.

Group II: 'Chronic', in which problems identified at the time of the overdoses had persisted for 1 month or more. Over half the adolescents were in this group.

Group III: 'Chronic with behaviour disturbance', which included adolescents

Table 4

Characteristics of adolescent self-poisoners who were categorized according to a simple classification scheme

	Classification		
	Group 1 'Acute'	Group 2 'Chronic'	Group 3 'Chronic with behaviour disturbance
Broken homes		+	+++
Family history of psychiatric disorder			+++
Poor relationship with parents: mother		+	+++
father	+	++	+++
Previous psychiatric disorder or treatment		+	+++
Previous overdose/ self-injury			++
Number of problems	+	++	+++
Psychiatric symptoms		+	+++

The + signs indicate extent to which a characteristic was displayed by members of each group.

for whom, as in Group II, current problems had persisted for a month or more, but who were distinguished from that group by having in addition recently shown some form of behavioural disturbance (e.g. severe truanting, stealing, or fighting). Just under a quarter of the subjects were in this group.

The extent of family relationship difficulties increased from Group I, through Group II to Group III (Table 4). A similar pattern was found regarding psychiatric history, previous attempts, and numbers of current problems. After their overdoses nearly all of those in Group I settled down whereas more of those in Group II, and most of those in Group III, continued to have problems. Half of Group III took further overdoses or injured themselves in the following year.

CONTACTS WITH HELPING AGENCIES BEFORE ATTEMPTS

Many people who deliberately poison or injure themselves have been in contact with potential helping agencies shortly before they carry out their acts (Hawton and Blackstock 1976; Bancroft *et al.* 1977). Contacts made with helping agencies by a sample of 141 such people in Oxford are shown in Table 5. The vast majority had been in contact with some form of helping agency within the previous month and over a half had been during the previous week.

Table 5

Time of last contact with helping agencies before self-poisoning or self-injury for 141 patients. Results are given as percentages

Helping agency	Contact made within 1 week	Contact made within 1 month
General practitioner	36	63
Psychiatrist	15	22
Social worker	10	22
Clergy and voluntary agency	13	23
Samaritans	4	6
Any agency	54	82

The agency most commonly contacted was the general practitioner (Hawton and Blackstock 1976). Fewer of the younger age group, especially young adolescents, had visited their general practitioner beforehand. Many of the people who visited their general practitioners were suffering from anxiety or depression associated with social and interpersonal difficulties. Psychotropic drugs, particularly tranquillizers and antidepressants, were often prescribed as a result of these visits. In many cases, these were the drugs used in deliberate self-poisoning not long after such visits. This was especially true of minor tranquillizers. Interestingly, of those who did not contact their general practitioner beforehand, 25 per cent said that he had been unhelpful in the past, or would be unsympathetic or disapproving of the patient's problems, and 17 per cent thought that he would have been too busy to deal with such problems. The potential role of general practitioners in the prevention of attempted suicide, especially deliberate self-poisoning, is discussed in Chapter 10.

In the study from Oxford (Bancroft *et al.* 1977), patients had far less often contacted agencies other than the general practitioner shortly before their overdoses, although it is noteworthy that almost a quarter had recently seen psychiatrists, and a similar proportion had seen social workers. Few patients had contacted the Samaritans, although most patients had heard of the organization. It seems that, as a group, people who contact the Samaritans when in distress have different characteristics from those who take overdoses (Kreitman and Chowdhury 1973*a*) and that this organization, despite the useful role it undoubtedly plays in helping people in distress, makes little contribution at present to the prevention of attempted suicide (p. 173).

MOTIVATIONAL ASPECTS OF SELF-POISONING

Recognition of the events and problems which have preceded attempts goes only part of the way to an understanding of the behaviour. A further important consideration concerns the motivational aspects of attempted suicide, which include the thoughts that precede attempts and the explanations given for the behaviour.

Premeditation

Many overdoses appear to involve little forethought. In a randomly selected series of 41 self-poisoners admitted to the general hospital in Oxford, two-thirds said they had thought about the act for less than an hour beforehand. A similar finding occurred when a consecutive series of 50 adolescent self-poisoners admitted to hospital were asked the same question. Attempts such as these are often described as 'impulsive'. This usually implies that a decision has been made with little or no planning or appraisal of the likely consequences. However, the individuals who make such attempts are probably prepared for the behaviour by their previous knowledge and experiences. Thus, for example, childhood thoughts such as 'You'll be sorry if I die' in response to being disciplined by parents, or knowing about attempts made by friends or relatives, or being aware of the behaviour through the media, may form attitudes about attempted suicide which increase the probability that an individual will resort to it as a means of coping when under severe stress. In addition, during the development of the current crisis there may have been earlier thoughts, however vague, about self-poisoning or self-injury. Thus, although an overdose, for example, might have been taken with only a couple of minutes of immediate forethought, considerable cognitive preparation may have occurred in the recent and distant past. Nevertheless, impulsive attempts often entail serious risks. For example, often the danger of the substances used and the likelihood of receiving help have not been considered. Alcohol consumption increases the likelihood of an impulsive attempt, through causing loss of control and disinhibition.

Where premeditation has occurred, especially if the action has been considered for days or even weeks beforehand, this is very often associated with serious suicidal intention.

Hopelessness

Pessimism about the future is a major factor in suicidal behaviour. Beck and colleagues (1975b) suggested that hopelessness might be the main symptom preceding suicide, and of greater importance in causing suicide than depression itself. Recently, he has reported empirical work supporting this hypothesis (Beck *et al.* 1985). Among attempted suicide patients it has also been shown that the extent of suicidal intent is significantly correlated with hopelessness, irrespective of the level of depression (Minkoff *et al.* 1973; Beck *et al.* 1975*b*; Wetzel *et al.* 1980; Dyer and Kreitman 1984).

Beck has also put forward the interesting idea that a sense of hopelessness arises out of activation of particular underlying cognitive schemata when an individual becomes depressed for whatever reason. These schemata are probably determined by early experiences, individuals therefore differing in the degree to which they are prone to developing pessimistic attitudes about the future, even when suffering from similar degrees of depression. Thus, an individual who experiences a high degree of hopelessness during an episode of depression is likely in a subsequent episode to experience a similar high degree of hopelessness, and therefore be at greater risk of suicidal behaviour than a depressed individual who does not become so pessimistic when depressed. This proposition has potential implications for the assessment of suicide risk (p. 64).

Explanations for attempted suicide

Many workers concerned with attempted suicide have neglected the explanations that people give for the behaviour. This is unfortunate because such explanations, both by patients and those involved in their care, can provide considerable assistance when trying to assess the motives underlying attempts. However, significant difficulties are encountered in research into this aspect of attempted suicide. As noted earlier, the behaviour is often viewed unfavourably by, in particular, physicians who provide resuscitative care for patients after overdoses (Ramon *et al.* 1975; Patel 1975; Ghodse 1978). Thus, when an individual gives an explanation for his own overdose this may be influenced by the attitudes he perceives in those around him. Similarly, the explanations given by those involved in a patient's care may also be moulded by their attitudes to the behaviour. For example, physicians (Ramon *et al.* 1975) and psychiatrists (Hawton *et al.* 1981*b*) are more favourably disposed towards patients whose attempts they perceive as being aimed at death, compared with those whose acts are seen as having a manipulative purpose.

Therefore, when investigating explanations for the behaviour it is important to remember that an individual's account will almost certainly be affected by his attitude to attempted suicide. Nevertheless, it is instructive to examine the types of explanations given by patients for their own behaviour, and the explanations given by psychiatrists. The views of psychiatrists are very important because during their clinical work with overdose patients they are likely to be trying to explain the behaviour and their explanations will provide the basis for important decisions concerning subsequent management.

In a study aimed at investigating this issue, 41 patients who had just taken overdoses were provided with a list of possible explanations for self-poisoning and asked to choose those which they thought best explained their overdoses (Bancroft *et al.* 1979). Subsequently, three psychiatrists were given details of clinical information, including transcriptions of interviews, for each of the patients and asked to choose explanations for each case from the same list. Just over a third of the patients indicated that they had wanted to die, a third that they did not mind either way, and just under a third said they had not wanted to die. The psychiatrists were in agreement with all the patients who denied any suicidal intention, but only agreed on suicidal intent for 53 per cent of the patients who said they had wanted to die. Whether this discrepancy was due to some patients selecting this reason because, although not really wanting to die, they recognized that this was a particularly acceptable explanation, or whether it was due to misunderstanding of the behaviour on the part of the psychiatrists, is unclear. However, many of the patients acted in a way which guaranteed survival and this therefore casts some doubt on their suicidal explanations.

The difference between self-poisoners themselves and psychiatrists in the attribution of suicidal intent for overdoses is of considerable interest. The reason why so many patients claim that they wanted to die may be related to the need of some to enhance the effect of the behaviour on others by communicating this message, and, perhaps, their need to justify the behaviour to themselves (Hawton 1982). Of course, in some cases the individuals will have had unequivocal suicidal intent. Such individuals form a relatively small group of those who are admitted to hospital having survived attempts.

The other explanations which the patients and psychiatrists were asked to choose from are shown in Table 6, together with the proportions of both groups choosing each of them. ('Situation so unbearable' was not included in the list offered to the psychiatrists.)

Table 6

Reasons chosen by patients (n=41) and psychiatrists to explain overdoses. Figures in parentheses are percentages

Reasons	Chosen by patients	Chosen by psychiatrists
1. The situation was so unbearable that you had to do something and didn't know what else to do*	23 (56)	—
2. Get relief from a terrible state of mind	18 (44)	16 (39)
3. Escape for a while from an impossible situation	13 (32)	6 (15)
4. You seemed to lose control of yourself and have no idea why you behaved that way	11 (27)	0
5. Show how much you loved someone	10 (24)	2 (5)
6. Make people understand how desperate you were feeling	8(20)	29 (71)
7. Seek help from someone	6 (15)	6 (15)
8. Find out whether someone really loved you	4 (10)	4 (10)
9. Frighten or get your own back on someone/make people sorry for the way they have treated you	4 (10)	29 (71)
10. Try to influence some particular person or get them to change their mind	3 (7)	22 (54)
11. Make things easier for others	3 (7)	0

*The psychiatrists were not offered this reason.

The patients' reasons included those selected by them as first, second, or third choice. The psychiatrists' reasons were those selected as likely in each case by at least two out of three psychiatrists.

The most surprising difference between the patients and psychiatrists was in their choice of 'hostile' and 'manipulative' reasons (9 and 10 in Table 6). Whereas these were some of the reasons least often indicated by the patients to explain their overdoses, they were among those most often chosen by the psychiatrists. The findings for the psychiatrists are congruent with the notable amount of interpersonal strife which characterizes close relationships for many people who take overdoses. Where the psychiatrists disagreed with patients concerning suicidal intent they nearly always chose one of these reasons. If an overdose is used as a means of evoking guilt in someone, or trying to modify his or her behaviour, presumably, as indicated above, the impact of the behaviour and its effectiveness will be enhanced if the act is perceived by that person as being largely suicidal [although, as noted earlier (p. 23), only anger appears to be increased by acts of high suicidal intent]. While several factors may influence such a perception, the patient's own explanation is likely to be an important one. At the same time, by saying that he wanted to die a patient may be enhancing the social acceptability of his behaviour.

A third finding from the study was the rarity with which both patients and psychiatrists selected the reason 'to seek help' to explain the behaviour. This is very surprising in view of the 'cry for help' explanation which is often given for self-poisoning (Stengel and Cook 1958). The psychiatrists often indicated a similar reason, 'to make people understand how desperate you were feeling'. However, as patients rarely chose either of these reasons, it appears that few patients thought they had been trying to elicit help by taking an overdose. This may, of course, be significant when considering subsequent management and may explain why an initial offer of help is so often rejected.

Two reasons which were chosen quite commonly both by patients and psychiatrists were 'to get relief from a terrible state of mind', and 'to escape for a while from an impossible situation'. Thus, self-poisoning often seems to be a means of reducing stress either by blotting out problems, presumably by becoming unconscious, or by a person ensuring that he will be physically removed from the situation.

Finally, it is important to recognize that there is more than one explanation for most overdoses. For example, an overdose of a tranquillizer may blot out intolerable distress, albeit temporarily, while ensuring that other people pay more attention to the self-poisoner's problems or change their behaviour towards the individual.

CONSEQUENCES OF THE BEHAVIOUR

The consequences of attempts are clearly extremely important. They can be separated into the consequences for the attempters themselves and the responses of other people around them. From what has already been noted concerning the common problems that precede attempts, it will be obvious that there will be a close relationship between the consequences for the attempters and the responses of other people. Nevertheless, for the present purpose it is easier to consider them independently.

Consequences for the individuals who make attempts

For many people who make attempts, rapid changes often occur and these are usually of a positive nature. These include changes both in social problems and in psychiatric symptoms, which are likely to be partly related to help that may be offered both by professional agencies, and by relatives and friends, as a consequence of an attempt. However, it is clear that the longer-term outcome for some patients is not good because they make repeat attempts, especially during the 3 months after an episode (Kessel and McCulloch 1966; Morgan *et al.* 1976; Bancroft and Marsack 1977).

Rapid improvement in social problems has been found to occur by 1–3 months after attempts (Hawton *et al.* 1981*a*). More than three-quarters of the patients included in a study comparing special treatment by social workers and traditional care reported after 4 months that there had been overall improvement in their social circumstances, although more of the group who received help from social workers showed such improvement (Gibbons *et al.* 1978*a*). When a group of 50 adolescent self-poisoners were followed up only 1 month after their overdoses, two-thirds were rated by research interviewers as showing improved adjustment (Hawton *et al.* 1982*b*). Of the more common problems faced by the adolescents at the time of their overdoses, those concerning boyfriends or girlfriends had the best outcome, whereas problems with school or work and those involving parents least often showed improvement.

The changes that may occur in psychiatric symptoms after attempts were assessed by Newson-Smith and Hirsch (1979*a*) using the Present State Examination (Wing *et al.* 1974) in their follow-up study of patients who had taken overdoses. Assessments carried out shortly after the overdoses, 1 week later and 3 months after the overdoses revealed that the proportions of patients reporting 'feelings of nervous tension' decreased from 75 to 41 to 28 per cent over the three interviews, 'depressed mood' from 73 to 37 to 24 per cent, and 'hopelessness' from 61 to 33 to 14 per cent. The considerable reduction found over the three assessments in terms of the proportions of patients who were suffering from psychiatric disorders were discussed earlier (p. 35).

The responses of other people

The immediate effects of attempts on other people were considered in the previous chapter. Some idea of the longer-term effects of attempts on other people was obtained in a follow-up study in Oxford of 45 patients interviewed between 6 and 9 months after their attempts (J. Smith, unpublished observations). Although the patients interviewed included only half of the original group, and therefore the results may be somewhat misleading, they do provide some interesting impressions of the types of responses to self-poisoning that may occur. The responses of other people can be separated usefully into those of the patients' partners, those of relatives, and those of friends and acquaintances.

Partners

In the slight majority of cases, the patients reported that the responses of their partners (spouse, boyfriend, or girlfriend) had been positive and sympathetic, and that improvement in the relationship occurred. For example, in one case a husband took an overdose after his wife's threats that she would leave him, and subsequently he said she had been very upset and 'wished she'd never made me take them' (the tablets). Ever since then the wife had been more settled.

In almost as many cases the reaction of partners had been negative, even hostile. Thus, one woman said of her husband's reaction after her overdose: 'He didn't say I should have come and explained things—he just said "You're lucky I let you in the house"—he gave me the impression he felt it was a shame I pulled round.'

Relatives

Near relatives were usually sympathetic, although often upset that the self-poisoner had not seen fit to come to them for help. Parents of adolescents, who probably often felt directly threatened by an attempt, tended to react with a mixture of anger and concern. One adolescent said that her father 'thought I was stupid—he kept me in for a week in the evenings and then let me out only at weekends'.

Friends and acquaintances

Friends and work-mates showed very little negative reaction, at least as far as was apparent to the self-poisoners. On the whole they were upset and sympathetic. Several patients commented that such people had been nicer to them since the overdose and had gone out of their way to help.

Clearly, the reactions of other people to the behaviour are of paramount importance, especially when the act has been carried out as a result of interpersonal strife. They may also play an important role in determining whether the behaviour is repeated. However, so far this has not been investigated systematically.

CONCLUSIONS

A wide range of problems and events precede attempted suicide. The most common constellation of difficulties consists of a recent serious argument or disruption of a relationship with a partner in the setting of longer-term relationship difficulties. Problems with children, employment (especially for men), and physical health, as well as psychiatric illness, are other important factors. Most adolescent self-poisoners have difficulties in their relationships with their parents, problems at school or with work, or in their relationships with boyfriends or girlfriends. Patients who make attempts have often visited their general practitioners shortly beforehand, and, if they take overdoses, often use the psychotropic medication prescribed during the visits.

Disentangling the motivation underlying attempted suicide involves complex issues. While premeditation often appears to be brief, it is likely that psychological reactions to earlier stresses may have provided some degree of cognitive rehearsal. The degree of hopelessness experienced by an individual may not only determine whether an attempt is made, but also the risk of eventual suicide.

One method of examining motivation is to compare the reasons given for the behaviour by suicide attempters with those given by other people. The explanations provided by patients differ in many respects from those of psychiatrists, a fact which should be borne in mind when assessing patients. The eventual consequences of an attempt will depend on many factors, but include how the behaviour is perceived by other persons in the attempter's social environment.

The first part of the book has provided a background for the second part, in which the major aim is to provide practical guidelines for the clinical management of patients who deliberately take overdoses or injure themselves.

PART II

The management of attempted suicide

In the previous two chapters the patterns of deliberate self-poisoning and self-injury, and the wide range of problems presented by patients involved in this behaviour, have been described. The reader should now be aware of the major position which attempted suicide occupies in terms of contemporary health care needs. The necessity for finding effective ways of management of the problem is all too apparent. The heterogeneity of difficulties faced by attempted suicide patients means that a wide range of treatment options should be available to meet patients' needs. Most have problems of a social kind, some have serious psychiatric disorders, and others have resorted to the behaviour in response to a transient crisis. Clearly a standard therapeutic response to such problems is not appropriate. In the second section of this book the range of treatment available will be described in detail.

However, before deciding what treatment is most appropriate, each case must undergo a thorough assessment. The variety of problems likely to be encountered, and the potential seriousness of the behaviour for the future welfare of patients, including the risk of repeat attempts and possible completed suicide, mean that assessment should be careful and extensive. Appropriate training must be provided for staff who take responsibility for the assessment. In addition, assessment should occur as soon as possible after an attempt; the situation in some hospitals in which a busy psychiatrist sees several patients at the end of a long day and only after social work reports have been prepared, thus necessitating several days' delay in some cases, is far from satisfactory. In the next chapter an approach to assessment is presented which it is hoped will be found useful by those engaged in such work or those responsible for planning services.

The treatment of attempted suicide patients after discharge from the general hospital is emphasized, because this aspect of patient care has received scant attention over recent years despite the increase in the number of patients requiring help. Three chapters are devoted to treatment, and include detailed description of the content of therapy. Case descriptions are used liberally in order to illustrate treatment methods and the problems that therapists commonly encounter. A separate chapter has been devoted to patients who injure themselves because they often require a different therapeutic approach compared with patients who take overdoses.

The extent of the problem of attempted suicide and the failure of traditional services to meet the needs of patients have meant that attention has recently turned to the organization of special services for attempted suicide patients. Important developments include the involvement of physicians, social workers, and nurses in management programmes where they work in collaboration with psychiatrists. This is encouraging because it is clear that psychiatrists cannot deal with all the problems of such patients and may indeed be inappropriate for some of them. A chapter has therefore been devoted to ways in which clinical services might be organized. This is not intended just for clinical services which have extensive staff resources, but includes guidelines which may assist those working in areas where the availability of staff poses strict limitations on the development of anything more than a minimal service.

Lastly, the very difficult issues of primary and secondary prevention of attempted suicide and its concomitant social and psychological problems are considered. It is hoped that the discussion of methods of prevention will encourage a positive approach to this important aspect of the problem of attempted suicide.

4

Assessment of patients after deliberate self-poisoning or self-injury

THE OBJECTIVES OF ASSESSMENT

Most individuals who are found to have taken overdoses or injured themselves are referred to casualty departments. A large proportion of these are then admitted to the general hospital for treatment and monitoring of the possible medical complications. The need for psychiatric evaluation arises after the patient has been seen by the casualty officer or while the patient is being treated in hospital.

The therapist who undertakes the psychiatric assessment of attempted suicide patients should try to answer the following questions (Table 7).

Table 7

Assessment of patients after deliberate self-poisoning or self-injury: the therapists' questions

---

1. What is the explanation for the attempt in terms of likely reasons and goals?
2. What was the degree of suicidal intent?
3. Is the patient at risk of suicide now, or is there an immediate risk of further overdose or self-injury?
4. What problems, both acute and chronic, confront the patient? Did a particular event precipitate the attempt?
5. Is the patient psychiatrically ill, and if so what is the diagnosis and how is this relevant to the attempt?
6. What kind of help would be appropriate, and is the patient willing to accept such help?

---

1. What is the explanation for the attempt in terms of likely reasons and goals?

Understanding why the person made the attempt is central to the whole assessment, although there are methodological and practical difficulties in doing so, as discussed in Chapter 3. However, it is important for the therapist to try to understand the attempt in terms of, first, the circumstances and expected consequences; secondly, why the attempt happened now, especially if the patient has suffered long-standing difficulties; and, thirdly, the reasons given by the patient for the act, including whether the patient wanted to die. At the same time, the therapist should try to assess whether the patient's account is consistent with his behaviour and the circumstances surrounding it, and whether the attempt appeared to have been directed at anyone in particular, or to have a specific goal. The actual consequences of the attempt and, especially, the response of the patient's partner or other significant family members should also be considered.

2. What was the degree of suicidal intent?

Although in many cases the act will not have been a determined attempt to end the person's life, the degree of overlap between patients who attempt suicide and those who kill themselves (p. 21) requires that careful consideration be given to evaluating to what extent the patient wanted to die, and what steps he had taken to ensure this outcome. The degree of suicidal intent at the time of the attempt may be crucial in deciding what kind of help to offer the patient.

3. Is the patient at risk of suicide now, or is there an immediate risk of further overdose or self-injury?

The presence of continuing risk of suicidal behaviour will also influence the choice of further help, particularly if the patient is at risk of completed suicide, in which case psychiatric inpatient care may have to be provided.

4. What problems, both acute and chronic, confront the patient? Did a particular event precipitate the attempt?

As we discussed in Chapter 3, most suicide attempters have suffered an accumulation of threatening life events in the weeks preceding the attempt, and the majority are expecting acute interpersonal and social difficulties against a background of chronic problems. Clarification of the precise nature of these problems and their relative contribution to the attempt is necessary before deciding what kind of help may be appropriate. Adequate assessment of the problems usually requires interviewing the patient's partner or other relatives, which is particularly important when the attempt followed a row or major disagreement.

5. Is the patient psychiatrically ill, and if so what is the diagnosis and how is this relevant to the attempt?

As was also discussed in Chapter 3, many suicide attempters show psychiatric symptoms, although only a minority of patients suffer from formal psychiatric disorders requiring psychiatric treatment. Establishing whether the patient is suffering from psychiatric disorder and the nature of such disorder will be very relevant to understanding the attempt, and deciding what type of further help is needed.

6. What kind of help would be appropriate, and is the patient willing to accept such help?

The assessment interview is principally geared towards establishing whether the patient needs further help to deal with the current situation, and making arrangement to provide such help. Many patients will welcome the opportunity of receiving counselling or other forms of help, but some may refuse any further contact. In these cases the therapist will have to decide whether the patient is making a rational and responsible decision or whether the patient's judgement is impaired by his problems or by the presence of psychiatric disorder. In a small minority of cases the patient may not be responsible for his actions and someone else may have to take responsibility, which could include compulsory psychiatric admission. The decision to take over responsibility from the patient can be a difficult decision to make and one that can be reached only after careful assessment.

While the principal aims of the assessment interview are to clarify the patient's current difficulties and to decide what help might be required, the interview should not be regarded as a mere fact-finding exercise leading to a rapid decision about disposal. The assessment can have considerable therapeutic effects, for example, by allowing the patient to express feelings or discuss problems which he had not been able to disclose before, or by helping him to understand his problems better. For some patients, this interview with the therapist will be the only contact with professional help they are prepared to accept, and it is therefore important to exploit its therapeutic possibilities, especially if a patient does not wish any further help or is unlikely to keep follow-up appointments.

The nature of the tasks facing the therapist involved in the assessment of attempted suicide patients means that he must possess adequate interviewing skills to encourage patients to talk about their difficulties and to elicit reliable information. At the same time, the therapist should have the knowledge to be able to evaluate the information obtained and make accurate judgements about, for example, the degree of suicidal intent, the presence of psychiatric disorder, or the risk of suicide. In the rest of this chapter, the setting of the interview and some general guidelines aimed at facilitating communication between patient and therapist will be described, followed by detailed discussion of how to fulfil the objectives of the assessment interview.

GENERAL ASPECTS OF THE ASSESSMENT INTERVIEW

Introduction

It should be clear from the description of the objectives of assessment that adequate coverage of these will be possible only if sufficient time is allowed, and if the interview takes place in appropriate surroundings. A hurried interview in a cubicle in the casualty department or in the open ward with nearby patients listening to the conversation is clearly not conducive to disclosure of personal problems and should be avoided. The therapist should, whenever possible, use a side room or office where the patient can be interviewed without interruptions.

The timing of the assessment is important. The patient should be interviewed as soon as he is fit to give a reliable account of the circumstances of his attempt. If a patient is interviewed when the psycho-pharmacological effects of the overdose or the medical treatment given for it are still present, the information given may be inaccurate or he may show symptoms which give a distorted picture of his mental state. On the other hand, if the interview takes place many hours or even days after admission, the crisis may appear to be over by the time the therapist becomes involved, thus preventing accurate understanding both of problems and the attempt. For example, the overdose may have caused the patient's partner to feel guilt and therefore she may have changed her behaviour towards the patient, whilst the basic problems in the relationship remain unchanged. This in turn may perpetuate the difficulties.

The therapist's own attitudes to attempted suicide patients may affect the interview and influence the kind of information that the patient is willing to give. As discussed in Chapter 2, negative attitudes to these patients are not uncommon amongst hospital staff (Ramon *et al.* 1975), and the quality of the assessment will probably suffer if the patient is regarded as 'just another overdose', or as someone occupying a medical bed under false pretences. It is important therefore that the therapist approaches the patient with a positive and open attitude to understanding his problems.

Interview schedule

During the interview the therapist will be trying to obtain fairly precise information from someone who is still in a distressed state. This means that the therapist has to proceed in a flexible way, allowing and even encouraging the expression of feelings by the patient, while at the same time gathering essential information, all within a reasonable period of time. Clinical and research experience (Hawton *et al.* 1979; Bancroft *et al.* 1979) have suggested that a semi-structured interview approach is very effective, without the disadvantages of either the 'check-list' or unstructured type of interviews. This approach, which can be used adequately both by doctors and by non-medically qualified therapists with appropriate training (Catalan *et al.* 1980*b*), differs from usual psychiatric history-taking in that it focuses specifically on understanding the attempt and clarifying the current problems faced by the patient, while incorporating some aspects of the traditional psychiatric interview, such as the examination of the mental state. Another important feature is that the patient is encouraged to take an active part in defining his problems and in discussing what treatment might be appropriate. The stages of the interview are summarized in Table 8.

Table 8

Stages in the assessment interview

Establishing rapport	Introduction by name and explanation of the purpose of the interview
Understanding the attempt	1. Detailed account of events in the 48 hours preceding the attempt 2. Circumstances surrounding the act—degree of planning, isolation, suicide note, reasons, actions after attempt, and whether alcohol was taken 3. Previous attempts
Clarification of current difficulties	1. Nature of problems and their duration, and recent changes 2. Areas to be covered—psychological and physical problems, relationship with partner and other family members, children, work, friends, and consumption of alcohol
Background	1. Relevant family and personal history 2. Usual personality
Coping	1. Current coping resources—personal resources and external resources (such as friends, social agencies, and GP) 2. Previous ways of coping with difficulties
Assessment of mental state at interview—especially mood and cognitive state	
List of current problems—formulated with patient	
Establishing what further help is required	1. What the patient wants and is prepared to accept 2. Who else should be involved (e.g. the partner or other relatives)
Contract	Terms of further involvement of the therapist or other agencies are made explicit and agreed

Establishing rapport with the patient

The initial contact with the patient can greatly influence the course of the interview and the nature of the information that the patient provides. Suicide attempters do not necessarily expect help and may not want to talk about their actions. Indeed, some will not have been told that a doctor or a member of the psychiatric team is coming to talk about their problems, and the unexpected arrival of such a person may suggest to the patient that he is considered mentally ill. At this stage of the interview it is important to establish a relationship which is positive and non-threatening, and to give the patient a chance to express any doubts or anxieties concerning the interview.

The therapist should introduce himself by name and professional role, and explain his presence by saying that the casualty officer or ward doctor has told him about the patient and that he is willing to try to help. If the patient is reluctant to talk it is important to point out that the assessment interview is a routine procedure, independent of whether the patient wants any further help, and that by the end of the interview the therapist and patient will be in a better position to decide jointly whether further contact is desirable. Some patients are reluctant to talk even after they have apparently accepted the therapist's presence. This problem is discussed later in this chapter (p. 77).

Good rapport is not necessarily maintained throughout the interview and the therapist should be aware of changes. These may be the result of the way questions are asked or because sensitive topics are broached. If changes in rapport occur the therapist should stop and explore the difficulties before continuing with the interview.

It may be useful to say at the beginning how long the interview is likely to take, while stressing that more time could be found at a later stage if necessary. In practice, 1 hour is usually sufficient for the initial assessment.

SPECIFIC ASPECTS OF THE ASSESSMENT INTERVIEW

The means of achieving the objectives listed at the beginning of the chapter will now be considered in detail.

Understanding the attempt and assessing degree of suicidal intent

Understanding why the patient attempted suicide is best achieved by asking the patient to give a detailed *sequential account of events* in the 48 hours preceding the attempt and the circumstances leading up to the hospital admission. After an opening question such as 'Can you tell me what happened in the 2 days before you came into hospital?', the therapist simply needs to return the patient to this topic when necessary and to ask for clarification if some detail of the account is not clear. A great deal of useful information about significant people in the person's environment and reasons for the act can be obtained in the course of such an account. Some patients tend to talk about the main problems without giving adequate information about the circumstances surrounding the attempt. This may occur because the problems are prominent in the person's mind or because the patient is reluctant to disclose details about the actual attempt which might be seen as unacceptable. Whatever the case, it will be useful to reassure the patient by explaining that sufficient time will be given to discussion of the problems, but that the therapist wishes to ask some more questions about the attempt first.

After obtaining the description of the events which appear to have precipitated the attempt, the therapist should concentrate on identifying the circumstances surrounding it, particularly to assess the *degree of suicidal intent*. To do this he will have to ask questions about the following.

1. Whether the attempt was impulsive or planned; if the latter, the duration of the plans.

2. Whether the patient was alone, or whether someone was present or within easy access.

3. Whether the patient was likely to be found soon after the attempt.

4. The nature of any precautions taken to prevent or ensure discovery.

5. The drugs taken, including the quantity, and whether other drugs were available but not taken; this includes the consumption of alcohol during or preceding the attempt.

6. The patient's expectation regarding the effect of the drugs or injury.

7. The presence of a suicide note or message, including tape-recorded statements.

8. The patient's efforts to obtain help after the attempt, and events leading to admission to hospital.

Table 9
Suicidal intent scale

I Objective circumstances related to suicide attempt

1. Isolation: 0 = somebody present; 1 = somebody nearby, or in visual or vocal contact; 2 = no one nearby or in visual or vocal contact

2. Timing: 0 = intervention probable; 1 = intervention unlikely ; 2 = intervention highly unlikely

3. Precautions against discovery/intervention: 0 = no precautions; 1 = passive precautions, e.g. avoiding others but doing nothing to prevent their intervention, alone in room with unlocked door; 2 = active precautions, e.g. locked door

4. Acting to get help during/after attempt: 0 = notified potential helper regarding attempt; 1 = contacted but did not specifically notify potential helper regarding attempt; 2 = did not contact or notify potential helper

5. Final acts in anticipation of death (e.g. will, gifts, insurance): 0 = none; 1 = thought about or made some arrangements; 2 = made definite plans or completed arrangements

6. Active preparation for attempt: 0 = none; 1 = minimal to moderate; 2 = extensive

7. Suicide note: 0 = absence of note; 1 = note written, but torn up, or thought about; 2 = presence of note

8. Overt communication of intent before the attempt: 0 = none; 1 = equivocal communication ; 2 = unequivocal communication

II Self-report

9. Alleged purpose of attempt: 0 = to manipulate environment, get attention, revenge; 1 = components of '0' and '2'; 2 = to escape, solve problems

10. Expectations of fatality: 0 = thought that death was unlikely: 1 = thought that death was possible, but not probable; 2 = thought that death was probable or certain

11. Conception of method's lethality: 0 = did less to self than thought would be lethal; 1 = was unsure if action would be lethal; 2 = equalled or exceeded what he thought would be lethal

Table 9. *cont.*

12. Seriousness of attempt: 0 = did not seriously attempt to end life; 1 = uncertain about seriousness to end life; 2 = seriously attempted to end life

13. Attitude toward living/dying: 0 = did not want to die; 1 = components of '0' and '2'; 2 = wanted to die

14. Conception of medical rescuability: 0 = thought that death would be unlikely with medical attention; 1 = was uncertain whether death could be averted by medical attention; 2 = was certain of death even with medical attention

15. Degree of premeditation: 0 = none, impulsive; 1 = contemplated for 3 hours or less before attempt; 2 = contemplated for more than 3 hours before attempt.

Beck *et al.* (1974*a*) have developed a scale (the Beck Suicidal Intent Scale) to help measure the degree of suicidal intent associated with an attempt. The scale, which is shown in Table 9, has two sections; the first covering the circumstances surrounding the attempt and the second concerning the patient's expectations and feelings at the time. It includes 15 items, and each one can be scored 0, 1, or 2. The total score (range 0–30) is used to assess the degree of suicidal intent. High scores correspond to higher suicidal intent. The scale is easily administered and can be incorporated conveniently into the clinical interview. Taken in isolation, intent scores would be only of limited value, but together with careful evaluation of the patient's problems and mental state, the Suicidal Intent Scale can be of great help to the therapist.

As was discussed in Chapter 3 (p. 41), when motivational aspects of attempted suicide were considered, the extent of suicidal intent as measures by the Beck Suicidal Intent Scale has been found to be more closely associated with the presence of feelings of *hopelessness*, rather than with the degree of depression (Minkoff *et al.* 1973; Beck *et al.* 1975*b*; Wetzel 1976; Dyer and Kreitman 1984). Feelings of *hopelessness* may therefore be one of the relevant contributing factors involved in the suicidal attempt, and may require specific attention during subsequent treatment. This is especially important in the light of the finding of Beck *et al.* (1985) that among depressed patients admitted to hospital with suicidal ideas, levels of hopelessness at the time of admission were a better predictor of risk of eventual suicide than was severity of depression (p. 41). A scale is available to evaluate hopelessness (Beck *et al.* 1974*b*). Examples of some items from this scale include: 'I look forward to the future with hope and enthusiasm; my future seems dark to me; when I look ahead to the future, I expect I will be happier than I am now; things just won't work out the way I want them to'. Patients are asked to say whether or not they agree with these statements. However, in routine clinical practice it is usually sufficient to enquire in detail about the individual's attitudes towards the future and the extent to which he thinks his problems can eventually be surmounted.

The relationship between suicidal intent and medical seriousness of the attempt is uncertain. While violent methods appear to be associated with high suicidal intent, in cases of self-poisoning low suicidal intent scores can be associated with high risk of medical complications (Fox and Weissman 1975). Although some authors have shown a correlation between suicidal intent and medical seriousness (e.g. Power *et al.* 1985), the main factor to consider when assessing suicidal intent in this respect is to what extent the individual was aware of the likely medical consequences of the attempt. Beck *et al.* (1975*a*) have demonstrated very clearly how suicidal intent correlates very highly with medical danger when the attempter is able to predict accurately the probable outcome of the act of self-harm, while the correlation between suicidal intent and medical danger is very low when the individual is not well-informed about the likely consequences. Paracetamol overdoses are a good example. Ingestion of large amounts of paracetamol carries serious risk of acute toxic hepatitis, but it is often taken impulsively by people who are unaware of its toxic effects (Gazzard *et al.* 1976).

Once the initial sequential account is reasonably complete, the therapist should ask direct questions to clarify the *reasons for the attempt*, while at the same time he should avoid suggesting particular reasons or implying criticism of the person's behaviour. For example, the therapist could ask questions such as: 'Can you explain why in the end you took the tablets?', 'What effect did you think it would have on other people?', 'How do you feel about it now?'. The reactions of the patient's partner and other relatives or friends should be noted, and the patient should be asked whether their response was what he would have expected. At some stage the therapist should ask *whether the patient wanted to die* at the time, and whether the patient still wishes to die now or regrets being alive.

At some point, the patient should be asked about any previous attempts, what led up to them and what were their consequences. The patient's account of attempts by relatives, friends, or other people known to him, as well as cases reported by the media, may also be informative. By the end of the assessment interview, the therapist should be able to decide whether the attempt is understandable in terms of the patient's problems and background. If the therapist feels unable to understand the attempt, he should ask himself why this might be so. For example, is it due to significant information remaining undisclosed because of the patient's fear of disapproval or continuing suicidal intentions, or is the patient suffering from a psychiatric disorder? Clarification of these issues is essential during assessment, and will virtually always require interviewing other informants, such as the patient's partner or relatives, and the general practitioner. This is discussed later in this chapter (p. 72).

Assessment of suicide risk

The therapist should be alerted to the possible risk of suicide if a patient says he wanted to die at the time of his attempt and if he continues to express suicidal ideas. In addition, there is evidence that the demographic characteristics of patients and the circumstances surrounding attempts can help to predict the risk of subsequent fatal attempts. Tuckman and Youngman (1968) followed up 3800 attempters and found that factors associated with subsequent suicide included: (i) age 45 years or more; (ii) male sex; (iii) being unemployed or retired; (iv) being separated, divorced, or widowed; (v) living alone; (vi) poor physical health; (vii) having received medical treatment within 6 months; (viii) psychiatric disorder, including alcoholism; (ix) having used violent methods such as hanging, shooting, jumping, or drowning; (x) presence of a suicide note; and (xi) history of previous attempts.

The risk of suicide increased in proportion to the number of predictors present. For example, attempters with two to five factors had a suicide rate of 6.98 per 1000, while those with ten or more had a suicide rate of over 60 per 1000. Tuckman and Youngman's scale correlates quite well with Beck's Suicidal Intent Scale (Pallis and Sainsbury 1976), although the former is concerned with risk of subsequent suicide and the latter is concerned with the severity of an attempt that has already occurred. Pierce (1981) has demonstrated that patients with high scores on a modified version of the Suicidal Intent Scale are at increased risk of subsequent suicide.

The value of combining information about the circumstances of the attempt and the demographic characteristics of the individual has been shown by Pallis and co-workers (Pallis *et al.* 1982, 1984; Pallis 1984), who demonstrated the predictive efficacy of a modified version of the Beck Suicidal Intent Scale, including seven items from the original scale (isolation, timing, precautions against discovery, actions to seek help, final acts in anticipation of death, degree of planning, presence of suicide note), used in conjunction with a six-item list consisting of data about the individual's age, sex, social class, work status, living arrangements, and suicidal communication in the last year. Items in Pallis's scale are given varying weights, and appropriate cut-off points are available to estimate the degree of suicidal risk (Pallis 1984). Two further factors which distinguish attempters who subsequently kill themselves from surviving attempters are the break-up of the relationship with a partner in the year before the attempt, and a major row during the 48 hours preceding the attempt, both being far less common in eventual suicides than survivors (Pallis *et al.* 1982; Hawton and Fagg, in preparation).

The importance of taking into consideration demographic factors and the circumstances surrounding the attempt becomes clear when dealing with 'failed suicides'. Such patients may deny any suicidal intention, but careful assessment of these factors should alert the therapist to the possible high risk of suicide.

It should be stressed, however, that the identification of individuals at risk of eventual suicide is essentially a clinical task. Predictive scales can be of value to clinicians, but the inevitable statistical limitations of such scales mean that they should not be used in isolation (Murphy 1984).

Assessment of risk of repetition

As discussed in Chapter 2, repetition of attempts is most likely to occur in the 3 months after an episode, and it is important to be able to identify those at risk at the time of assessment. Buglass and

Horton (1974) identified factors which distinguish repeaters from non-repeaters, and devised a simple scale to predict the risk of a further attempt. It includes six items: (i) problems in the use of alcohol; (ii) diagnosis of sociopathy ('predominant distress of the patient's situation falls on society'); (iii) previous inpatient psychiatric treatment; (iv) previous outpatient psychiatric treatment; (v) previous self-poisoning or self-injury resulting in hospital admission; and (vi) not living with relatives. A patient is given one point for each item applicable to him. The higher the score, the greater the risk of repetition. The items are rather crude and in some cases ('problems in the use of alcohol', 'sociopathy') difficult to define precisely, but Buglass and Horton found that a patient scoring nought had a probability of repetition within 1 year of 5 per cent, while a patient with a score of 5 or 6 had a repetition probability of 48 per cent. Therefore, the scale can be particularly useful in identifying patients at very high risk of repetition.

Further attempts by some individuals may be characterized by an increase in suicidal intent (as evaluated by the Suicidal Intent Scale). Such individuals are more likely to be under the age of 35, compared with non-repeaters or with repeaters who do not show an increase in suicidal intent. Also, compared with non-repeaters, they are more likely to be males. Patients who repeat with rising intent have a higher risk of suicide in the long-term and they are therefore a group that requires special attention (Pierce 1984).

Patients whose problems and general circumstances have not altered significantly as a result of an attempt are at risk of further episodes in the immediate or near future. This is so particularly when the patient's stated or implicit goals have not been realized, as in the case of a man whose wife refuses to return to him despite his admitting that he took the overdose as a means of putting pressure on her to come back. In such cases there may be a risk of the patient taking a further and perhaps more serious overdose to try to obtain the desired response. Chronic repeaters present special difficulties and they are discussed later in this chapter (p. 79).

Assessment of current problems

During the sequential account of the circumstances preceding the attempt, the patient will have provided quite a lot of information about the problems he was experiencing at the time. The therapist should now take each of the problems in turn and clarify the precise nature of the difficulties, including when and how the problem started. He must also determine how the various problems related to each other. Clarification of problems sometimes may require asking about the patient's background and earlier experiences, so that a more complete picture of his life begins to emerge.

Sometimes, it is difficult to decide when to stop exploring a particular problem. Some patients may give unnecessary detail or numerous examples of previous incidents which are all closely similar. Others, such as a woman who has been raped, may find it too threatening or distressing to talk about the problems in detail. The important thing is to understand how the attempt and a particular problem may be related, and in order to achieve this, exhaustive information may not be essential at this stage. Further clarification can occur later, especially after discussion with other informants.

Once the problems spontaneously mentioned by the patient have been explored, the therapist should ask about other potential problem areas. As an aid, it is useful to have a mental check-list of problem areas, including the following.

1. Relationship with partner or spouse.
2. Relationship with other family members, particularly young children.
3. Employment or studies.
4. Financial matters.
5. Housing.
6. Legal, including impending court proceedings.
7. Social isolation, relationships with friends.
8. Use of alcohol and drugs.
9. Psychiatric health.
10. Physical health.
11. Sexual adjustment.
12. Bereavement and impending loss.

Excessive drinking is not an uncommon problem amongst attempted suicide patients. Therefore, the therapist should always ask about alcohol consumption. Sometimes patients may be reluctant to disclose how much they drink or what effect alcohol has on them, and the therapist may need to ask more general questions about the patient's intake. Mayfield *et al.* (1974) have shown that a short questionnaire of only four questions can be used to identify most psychiatric patients who are alcoholic. The four questions are:

1. 'Have you ever felt you should cut down on your drinking?'
2. 'Have people annoyed you by criticizing your drinking?'
3. 'Have you ever felt bad or guilty about your drinking?'
4. 'Have you ever had a drink first thing in the morning to steady your nerves or get rid of a hangover?'

Mayfield and co-workers showed that by taking two positive answers as criterion, they identified 81 per cent of alcoholic patients and misclassified as alcoholic only 11 per cent of non-alcoholics. Although the questionnaire's use with overdose patients has not been subjected to systematic evaluation, the four questions might serve as a useful introduction to assessing alcohol abuse.

Many overdose patients are confused and overwhelmed by their difficulties; the process of discussing and defining the problems together with the therapist can be of therapeutic value. This can be enhanced further by encouraging the patient to formulate his difficulties in the form of a *problem list*, which will assist both therapist and patient in deciding what problems require consideration now and what kind of help is necessary for each of them. The formulation of the problem list is a crucial point in the interview. Until now the therapist has been asking questions and encouraging the patient to disclose information in order to build up a picture of the current crisis and, in some ways, the therapist has taken a more active role than the patient, directing the interview and focusing on specific aspects of recent events. At this point, however, the therapist should begin to hand over responsibility to the patient; the first step in this direction is to ask the patient to define and summarize what he regards as the present problems. The patient may not necessarily see as problems some of the difficulties discussed in the interview, perhaps because they have been accepted as inevitable or because they are of less relevance than the therapist might have thought. On the other hand, particular aspects of the crisis which have been discussed only in passing may cause the patient more concern than the therapist realised at first. In addition, the formulation of a problem list makes the task of dealing with the crisis easier by breaking it down into specific problems that can then be tackled in turn. It also makes it easier for the therapist to evaluate subsequently the effectiveness of the help he has provided.

The problem list should be arrived at by joint discussions

between patient and therapist, and as far as possible, should be based on what the patient regards as problems. Sometimes there may be a clear discrepancy between what the patient and the therapist see as problems. An example is in the case of someone who claims that drink is not a problem for him, but who shows clear symptoms of addiction to alcohol. In such cases the therapist should make his views clear and try to reach agreement with the patient that at least they will examine the problem at a later stage.

The majority of patients respond well to a request for the formulation of a problem list. However, in some cases the therapist may find it difficult to obtain the patient's co-operation; for example, the very severely depressed patient, or the patient who denies any problems and where the attempt remains unexplained. In such cases the therapist may have to construct his own problem list, which may include a diagnostic formulation or the therapist's inability to understand the attempt. Examples of problem lists are given in Chapters 6 and 7.

Assessment of psychiatric disorder

The therapist who assesses suicide attempters should be able to carry out a mental state examination with confidence. The evaluation of the mental state begins with the first contact with the patient and continues throughout the interview. However, it may be necessary to carry out a systematic examination of the mental state at some stage of the interview. This is best done after good rapport has been established and the patient has been able to express his feelings and discuss his problems at some length. Ideally, the questions about mental state should be incorporated as far as possible into the rest of the interview. Guidelines for the assessment of mental state are provided in Appendix I at the end of this chapter.

Formal mental state examination will be indicated if the patient's history suggests that he is suffering from a psychiatric disorder such as depression, alcoholism, schizophrenia, or dementia. The therapist should be alert particularly to symptoms suggesting severe depression (e.g. persistent low mood which is worse in the early part of the day, feelings of hopelessness, loss of appetite, loss of weight, early morning wakening, nihilistic ideas, lack of energy, suicidal ideation).

Sometimes it will be necessary to assess the patient's mental state early in the interview, particularly if there is some suggestion that the patient's cognitive functions remain affected by toxic effects of the substances ingested. It is important to be sure that the patient is orientated, that his memory for recent events is not impaired and that his concentration is reasonably normal, before embarking on extensive information gathering. If there is any doubt about these functions the therapist should stop and explain that he would like to make sure that the effects of the overdose are not making it difficult for the patient to give a clear account. Should the patient show evidence of cognitive impairment due to drug intoxication, it would be advisable to delay further assessment until the drug effects have worn off.

Staff on the medical ward can provide invaluable information about the patient's mental state, his reactions to visitors, and to the care being given to him.

Assessment of coping resources

Adequate assessment should also include discussion of the patient's strengths and resources both at the present time and in the past. This can best be done by considering coping resources under three headings:

1. *External resources and supportive relationships*—Who does the patient turn to when in trouble? Is there a confidant or close friend the patient can discuss his problems with? Is the general practitioner seen as potentially helpful and is there a social worker or health visitor already involved? Has the patient made use of any local self-help groups or associations? What would be his attitude if any of these agencies were to become involved now?

2. *Personal resources*—Does the patient have confidence in himself? What are his assets and strengths? What things is he good at? Can he suggest ways of tackling the present difficulties?

3. *Previous ways of coping*—How has the patient dealt with important changes in his life, such as leaving school, changing jobs, leaving home, marriage, childbirth, or death in the family? Are there examples of successful coping in the past?

Interviewing relatives and other informants

The assessment of suicide attempters should not be based solely on the patient's account of the attempt. Information from the patient's partner or other relatives should always be sought before the patient leaves hospital, particularly when the reasons for the attempt cannot be understood clearly. Before interviewing relatives, the therapist should discuss this with the patient and obtain his agreement. This is given readily in most cases. However, if a patient refuses to let the therapist talk to a relative or another informant he will have to decide whether complying with the patient's wishes carries a serious risk of missing important information which, if known, would indicate, for example, that the patient intends to kill himself.

It is best to interview relatives on their own first in order to obtain their version of the circumstances and their response to the attempt without the editing that the patient's presence might produce. An interview room or office should be used to ensure privacy. The patient's spouse or partner is very often the person the overdose is aimed at, and so she may show feelings of guilt or anger which will help the therapist to understand the reasons for the act. It may also become clear what the relative's future intentions are, and whether she is willing to be involved in counselling. The patient's general practitioner should be contacted before reaching a decision about further treatment. He is likely to know the patient and be familiar with his difficulties, and he may provide valuable information. In addition, it is useful to discuss with the doctor the treatment alternatives available and to establish whether he is willing to be directly involved in helping with the patient's current problems.

Establishing what further help is required

In considering what care to offer the patient after assessment, the therapist will have to make a clinical decision concerning a fundamental question: can the patient take responsibility for himself or does responsibility need to be taken for him by someone else on a temporary basis? Often this can be a difficult decision to make and one that may require discussion with other therapists or colleagues. The patient's capacity to make rational judgements and take responsibility for himself can be affected not only by the presence of formal psychiatric disorder, such as severe depression or schizophrenia, but also by severe and persistent distress after adverse events, like bereavement and other forms of threatened or actual loss. In these cases the therapist or the patient's relatives may have to take responsibility for the patient, and this can mean psychiatric inpatient care, which sometimes may be against the patient's wishes. Most patients will be considered capable of taking responsibility for their own actions, and any further help provided by the therapist or others will depend on the patient's willingness to accept it, and will be determined by the nature of the patient's problems.

There is no universal agreement about how best to treat attempted suicide patients, and in view of the diversity of problems they present, management should be tailored as far as possible to suit each patient's needs. The range of general types of treatment available is illustrated in Table 10, which summarizes the forms of care offered during a 5-year period (1980–84) to 3457 consecutive patients referred to the emergency service dealing with attempted suicide patients in the general hospital in Oxford.

Table 10

Type of care offered to 3457 attempted suicide patients referred to the emergency service in the general hospital in Oxford during 1980–84. Results are given as percentages

Outpatient counselling (including a small proportion offered domicilary counselling):	
Emergency service	30.7
Referred to psychiatric hospital	13.3
Psychiatric inpatient care	6.3
Psychiatric day-patient care	2.6
Discharged to care of general practitioner	31.3
Other form of care (e.g. social services, voluntary agencies)	13.5
Self-discharge without arrangements for care	2.2

There are no absolute indications for one or other form of treatment, except perhaps in the case of patients suffering from severe psychiatric illness who are also at immediate risk of suicide. As in the case of other psychiatric or social problems where a decision concerning management has to be made, it is best to provide a set of guidelines on how to treat particular problems so that the therapist can make an informed choice when dealing with specific patients.

Outpatient counselling will be indicated for patients deemed capable of taking responsibility for themselves, whose problems are of moderate intensity and where the risks of suicide or immediate repetition are relatively small. Patients likely to benefit from this form of care include women and patients of both sexes experiencing dyadic problems (Hawton *et al.* 1987). Patients with family problems and those who have suffered a loss, or who are experiencing material and practical difficulties (employment, financial, housing, etc.) are also candidates for such help.

Domiciliary counselling may be indicated in some cases, particularly those with family problems or during the initial stages of outpatient counselling. The management of patients thought to require outpatient or domiciliary care is discussed in Chapter 5.

Psychiatric inpatient care will be indicated in patients who are unable to take responsibility for themselves, even with extensive support from others. This group is likely to include: (i) patients suffering from severe psychiatric disorder, especially depression; (ii) patients at immediate risk of suicide or repetition of the attempt; and (iii) patients who require a short period of removal from stress, such as those who face severe problems which have not improved as a result of the attempt or are likely to get worse, or when the patient's coping resources are exhausted, and he lacks the support of family and friends. This group is relatively small, but it is very important to identify these patients in view of the risks of inappropriate treatment. The management of patients requiring psychiatric inpatient treatment is discussed in detail in Chapter 7.

The majority of patients requiring inpatient care are willing to go into hospital voluntarily, but some may resist admission. In these cases the possibility of using a compulsory order of the Mental Health Act will have to be considered. It is usually very apparent when such a decision has to be made. This is often the case for patients who refuse help but are clearly suffering from serious depression with loss of insight, and those judged to be at risk of suicide who cannot give satisfactory assurance about their intentions. Similarly, there is usually little doubt in the case of a patient with acute schizophrenic illness or one suffering from a severe organic condition. However, in a few cases the decision is one of the most difficult to make in psychiatric practice. Discussion with a colleague is to be recommended in such circumstances. The clinician should also discuss the situation with the patient's relatives and a social worker. Whenever a clinician decides that compulsory admission is necessary he will need to communicate this to the patient in a sympathetic yet firm fashion. For a detailed discussion of the ethical issues which may be involved in compulsory hospitalization in relation to suicide risk, the reader is referred to the relevant chapters in the book edited by Bloch and Chodoff (1981).

This is not the place for a detailed description of all aspects of the 1983 Mental Health Act. However, to assist the reader, particularly one unfamiliar with the Act, a summary of those sections concerned with admission of patients to hospital or detention of patients already in hospital which are needed at times for attempted suicide patients in provided in Appendix II at the end of this chapter.

Day-patient care may be a useful half-way measure for patients with few external supports and whose problems have changed little with the attempt. In addition to having individual sessions with a therapist, the patient may join group activities (problem-solving groups, role play, art therapy). Day care can be followed by outpatient counselling. When considering what kind of help to offer outpatients and day patients, the therapist should be familiar with the type of patients likely to benefit from each form of treatment (e.g. individual therapies, marital counselling, sex therapy, family therapy), and with the resources available locally. This does not mean that he should necessarily be an expert in psychotherapy, psychopharmacology, or social work, but that he must possess a good understanding of the indications and limitations of the different techniques and treatments.

Discharge to the care of the general practitioner may be the best course of action when the attempt has been impulsive in nature, the patient's problems are minor and he feels capable of coping with them, with or without support from relatives or friends. Return to the general practitioner may also be indicated in more complicated cases when this is the choice of both the general practitioner and the patient, particularly if the doctor is already involved and is familiar with the patient's background and circumstances. Patients already in contact with other agencies (psychiatrists, social work departments, and counselling services) can usually be referred back after discussion with the individuals concerned. Some patients may need referral to *specialized units* for alcoholism or drug addiction. Others may benefit from referral to self-help groups, or Marriage Guidance, especially if the therapist is unable to offer counselling himself.

Open access to the therapist or other emergency staff by telephone can be a valuable aid for some patients offered outpatient care or for those who are returned to the general practitioner. In these cases the therapist would discuss the use of open access as one of the ways of coping with problems in the future, especially when the situation is becoming unmanageable or if the patient is at risk of making another attempt. Open access is discussed further in Chapter 5.

Contract

If the therapist is going to see the patient again, the terms of any further contact should be defined as precisely as possible. This will involve, for example, agreeing on what problems therapist and patient will work on, and whether the patient's partner or other people will also be attending. A provisional number of counselling sessions should be fixed, as well as their frequency and venue. The possibility of having access to the therapist between sessions should be discussed, as well as the use of other helping agencies such as the general practitioner.

PATIENTS PRESENTING SPECIAL PROBLEMS

While most patients welcome the possibility of discussing their problems and respond readily to the therapist's questions, some attempted suicide patients are unwilling to do so or present other difficulties which may test the therapist's skills and sensitivity. The examples included here are not a comprehensive list of such patients, but are intended to illustrate some of the difficulties that therapists may encounter and to suggest ways of dealing with them.

Patients who refuse to be interviewed

A patient who has taken an impulsive overdose for which he now feels ashamed may not wish to talk about it. Similarly, a person who has failed in a serious suicidal attempt and still intends to kill himself may be reluctant to discuss his actions. Some patients may feel threatened by the prospect of a psychiatric interview because of concern about being regarded as mentally ill, or because of fears about confidentiality or psychiatric inpatient admission. It is important for the therapist to reassure the patient, and to explain his role and his willingness to help. If despite this the patient still refuses to talk, it will be essential for the therapist to obtain information from other informants and from the general practitioner before the patient can be discharged. Compulsory detention in hospital will have to be considered when the patient's mental state at interview and the evidence concerning the attempt obtained from other sources suggest the presence of severe psychiatric disorder or serious suicide risk. When this is not the case and the patient is discharged home after incomplete assessment, the therapist might offer open access, or write to the patient a few days later reiterating his willingness to help.

Patients threatening discharge

A patient who did not envisage that his overdose would bring him to hospital may wish to leave before a proper assessment has been carried out. Such a patient is likely to be defensive and have poor rapport with the therapist. On the other hand, a patient who seriously intends to kill himself also may behave in this way. It is therefore important to try to rule out the possibility of serious suicide risk and presence of psychiatric disorder before the patient leaves the hospital. If the therapist has sufficient evidence to indicate that the patient is at immediate risk of suicide or requires urgent psychiatric treatment then authority to prevent the patient from discharging himself can be obtained under Section 5(2) of the Mental Health Act (1983), which applies to patients already in hospital. Details are given in Appendix II at the end of this chapter.

Patients refusing further help

A patient who has agreed reluctantly to be interviewed may well turn down the therapist's offer of further help. The therapist's response will depend on whether he regards the patient as capable of making such a decision. An example of this kind of situation is presented by the failed 'rational suicide'; that is, the patient who has made a determined, but unsuccessful attempt to end his life and who appears not to be suffering from psychiatric disorder at the time of the interview, but who still maintains his wish to kill himself in the future. Such patients are often elderly people with failing physical powers who are afraid of becoming a burden to others, or who fear pain or loneliness. It is essential for the therapist to rule out hidden psychiatric disorders, such as 'masked' or 'smiling' depression, and to explore ways of improving the patient's quality of life. The problems should be discussed with a senior psychiatrist, the patient's relatives, and also agencies involved in his care such as the general practitioner, social services, and health visitors. It is important to reiterate the therapist's offer of help, including open access, and if the patient is discharged it may be useful to write a few days later to remind him of the therapist's willingness to help.

The chronic repeater

Although small in number, chronic suicide attempters put great pressure on services and tend to antagonize people involved in their care. The results of psychiatric intervention are often disappointing, which contributes to the negative attitudes towards them. It is possible that, for some patients, psychiatric help reinforces repetition, and therefore it is important to be aware of this risk and deal with the patient in a way that does not make repetition more likely. For example, it may be advisable to ensure that the same therapist is involved after each attempt to allow the development of a therapeutic relationship and continuity of care. The patient should be encouraged to seek help before the problems become too severe and to use open access. The therapist may also offer to see the patient at length only if he does *not* repeat, rather than after an attempt. This is discussed further in Chapter 5 (p. 106).

The survivor of a suicide pact

Very occasionally, a patient admitted after a suicide attempt will be the surviving partner of a suicide pact. Such a patient can present special clinical and legal problems to the therapist involved in his psychiatric assessment. Careful evaluation should be made to exclude a psychiatric disorder, such as severe depression and schizophrenia, or symptoms suggestive of *folie à deux*. Psychiatric inpatient care will usually be indicated for treatment of psychiatric illness, or to give the patient time to deal with the aftermath of the attempt, especially grief concerning the partner's death. The possibility of compulsory admission to a psychiatric unit will have to be considered when the patient refuses further help and there is obvious risk of subsequent suicide. The reader is referred elsewhere (Parry-Jones 1973; Rosen 1981) for a more detailed review of the clinical and legal issues.

The patient at risk of delayed complications

Patients are sometimes at risk of late complications from their overdoses, which may prove fatal. This may occur, for example, after overdoses of paracetamol or paraquat. Such patients have often attempted suicide impulsively and with no suicidal intent, unaware of the possible disastrous consequences (Gazzard *et al.* 1976). One example was a 28-year-old single woman who was admitted to a general hospital one day at 9.00 a.m. having taken an overdose of 50 paracetamol and a few epanutin and phenobarbitone tablets at 11.00 p.m. the previous evening. She had suffered from epilepsy since childhood, although this was well controlled by anticonvulsants. Recently, she had experienced bouts of depression, which were becoming increasingly severe. On the evening she took the overdose she had been discussing her difficulties with a friend, but felt afterwards that she had been a burden, which made her feel even worse. On getting back to her flat she took the overdose impulsively, never having done anything like that before. She was found the next morning by her friend who telephoned and became concerned at getting no reply.

Her drowsiness lifted shortly after admission to hospital where she was assessed by a member of the psychiatric service. She denied any wish to die, but said she had wanted a temporary respite from her problems. Her score on the Beck Suicidal Intent Scale was low and she had no knowledge of the potential hazards of taking an overdose of paracetamol.

The next day she became jaundiced. It was clear that she had extensive liver damage. The therapist saw her several times to provide support and encouragement, but was also realistic with her about the situation. Her parents were seen regularly for support and kept closely informed of her clinical progress. Three days later her condition had deteriorated and she was transferred to the specialist unit for liver disease in another hospital, where she died after a further 10 days. The cause of death was hepatic failure due to paracetamol overdose with renal failure, cerebral oedema, intra-abdominal bleeding, and aspiration pneumonia. A verdict of death by suicide was recorded at the coroner's inquest. The therapist continued to see her parents after her death to provide support during their very intensive grief (Kingston and Hawton 1977). Cases such as these are likely to put great pressure on the therapist, who may need support from other members of the team.

The very young

Children and adolescents are likely to regard the therapist as an authority figure, which can inhibit such patients or cause them to give distorted information. The fact that they are usually experiencing problems with their parents or other grown-ups will tend to make matters worse. Special care and skills will be necessary to put the patient at ease and encourage trust. In some cases a young therapist may be preferable. The problems of children and adolescents who take overdoses or injure themselves were discussed in detail in Chapter 3.

CONCLUSIONS

The assessment of patients who have made suicide attempts is an essential part of their management. It should not be a perfunctory procedure, and the therapist should ensure that sufficient time is available to carry out an adequate assessment. The objectives of such an assessment include understanding the reasons why the attempt was made, assessing the degree of suicidal intent at the time of the act and the degree of hopelessness, evaluating the risk of suicide or a further attempt, clarifying the patient's problems, and establishing whether he is suffering from a psychiatric disorder. In addition, the therapist will have to determine whether the patient is capable of taking responsibility for himself or whether someone else should assume responsibility for the patient. The factors which should be considered when making this decision have been discussed. The therapist and patient will also have to decide what form of help may be appropriate to deal with the current problems and to prevent further attempts. The indications for the various forms of help available have been considered. Finally, examples have been given of problems which may occur during assessment.

APPENDIX I

Notes on the examination of mental state at interview

Assessment of mental state includes: (i) observation of a patient's behaviour and evaluation of his spontaneous comments throughout the interview; and (ii) asking direct questions to test mental function.

Because of possible persistent pharmacological effects of the overdose, it is important for the therapist to reassure himself at an early stage that the patient is orientated, can concentrate and has intact memory. If there is any suggestion of disorientation, confusion, or memory loss, it is important to establish their extent by direct questioning. Mental state examination includes the following areas of assessment.

1. Appearance

The patient's general appearance (dress, grooming and make-up), facial expression (sadness, anger, or distress), posture, and non-verbal responses to the therapist's presence (e.g. avoidance of the interviewer's gaze).

2. Manner and behaviour

Agitation or retardation of movement, alertness, or disinhibition, hostility or evasiveness. Abnormalities of movement and the presence of tremor or agitation may accompany disturbances of mood.

3. Speech

The amount, flow, and content of the patient's talk, as well as his expression, will give the therapist some idea of the patient's mood and general intellectual abilities. Hesitations or contradictory statements may suggest that an emotionally significant topic is being discussed. The content of the patient's talk, in particular, will help to assess his mood and detect the presence of abnormalities.

4. Mood

The main abnormalities of mood found in attempted suicide patients are *depression* and *anxiety*.

In addition to the information provided by non-verbal cues (appearance, manner, and behaviour) and the content of spontaneous speech, the therapist should assess the patient's mood by direct questioning, for example: 'How do you feel in your spirits?', 'How do you feel about the future?' (to elicit any feelings of hopelessness), 'Who or what do you feel is responsible for your problems?' (to assess the presence of feelings of guilt). In mental state examination of attempted suicide patients the therapist should always ask about suicidal ideas and intentions, including 'Did you want to die?', 'Do you regret surviving?', and 'Do you still feel you want to die?'

Questions should be asked about possible anxiety and tension. For example, 'Do you find yourself feeling anxious or tense for no good reason?', 'Are there any situations that make you feel particularly anxious or panicky?' The therapist should note whether the patient's appearance and behaviour are in keeping with his answers concerning his mood, and also whether the patient's mood remains constant during the interview.

Although not strictly part of the mental state examination, the presence of depressed mood should lead the therapist to ask questions about changes in functions which can be impaired by abnormal mood—namely appetite, weight, sleep, energy, and interest in sex. Any variation in mood throughout the day should also be noted.

5. Thought processes

The therapist should pay attention to the *speed, structure, content,* and *possession* of the patient's thought. Slow or retarded thinking accompanies depressive mood, while the opposite can be found in anxious or elated patients. The logical structure of the patient's thinking may be impaired, resulting in incoherent or bizarre thinking, with inappropriate or silly associations of words and concepts. This is particularly likely to occur in schizophrenia. When such disturbances occur, it is very helpful to write down a sample of the patient's speech. The content of the patient's thinking may include ideas of reference and delusional thinking. Delusions are false, unshakeable beliefs which are out of keeping with the patient's sociocultural background. Common delusions include those of persecution, bodily change, grandiosity, and worthlessness. They occur, for example, in schizophrenia, affective disorders, and drug-and alcohol-induced states. Abnormalities of the possession of thought include thought broadcasting (the patient complains that his thoughts are shared by people around him), thought blocking (sudden interruption in the flow of his thoughts), and passivity experiences such as thought insertion and thought withdrawal. All of them are typical of schizophrenia.

6. Cognitive functions

This involves assessment of the *level of consciousness, orientation, concentration,* and *memory*. Impairment in these functions can be due to the substances ingested or the treatment received, or it may be due to a more persistent and long-standing disturbance.

Orientation—The therapist should test the patient's orientation in time, place, and person, as well as the circumstances of the interview.

Concentration—The flow of the conversation and the way the patient answers questions will indicate to what extent he can maintain a particular course of thinking. Concentration can be tested by asking the patient to subtract serial sevens from a hundred, asking him to name the months of the year backwards, or by asking him to repeat a series of digits after the interviewer forwards (normal span = 6–7) and backwards (normal span = 4–5). It should be noted that serial sevens also tests mathematical ability and that digit span tests both concentration and immediate registration.

Memory—Short-term memory can be tested by asking about recent events that can be corroborated (visitors, meals, etc.). Registration, retention, and recall can be tested by giving the patient a name and address asking him to repeat them immediately (registration) and again after 5 minutes (retention and recall). Long-term memory can be tested by asking about significant dates in the patient's life (birth dates, marriage, and anniversaries) or past events generally known (dates of the Second World War, names of prime ministers, etc.).

General intellectual functioning—The patient's level of intellectual functioning can be estimated by reference to his interests, employment, educational achievements, and general information.

7. Perceptual functions

The main perceptual abnormalities are *illusions* and *hallucinations*.

An illusion is a misperception of an actual stimulus. Illusions are usually given a frightening or threatening interpretation. They are common in anxiety and depressive states, or if the patient is under considerable stress or in unusual surroundings.

Hallucinations are false perceptions without an external stimulus. They are usually of an auditory or visual nature. Auditory hallucinations of particular kinds occur in schizophrenia (e.g. voices talking about the patient) and depression (e.g. voices accusing the patient), while visual hallucinations often occur in organic states and drug intoxication. They may follow an overdose of tricyclic antidepressants. The patient's behaviour and speech may suggest that he is experiencing hallucinations. Direct questioning may also help elicit the presence of abnormal perception. For example, the patient may be asked about whether he has noticed any unusual experiences involving voices or visions.

8. Insight

Insight refers to the patient's ability to recognize that he is ill if he is suffering from a psychiatric illness. Insight may be impaired, for example, in schizophrenia, severe depression, hypomania, and organic brain syndromes.

APPENDIX II

Summary of sections of the Mental Health Act (1983) likely to be required for admission of attempted suicide patients

Section 2: Admission for assessment

Applicant—(i) Nearest relative; or (ii) approved social worker.

Medical recommendation—Two are required: (i) a medical practitioner (preferably with previous acquaintance of the patient; and (ii) a medical practitioner approved by the Regional Health Authority.

Grounds—(i) The patient is suffering from mental disorder of a nature or degree which warrants detention for assessment (or for assessment followed by medical treatment) for at least a limited period; and (ii) detention is required for the patient's health or safety, or for the protection of other persons.

Duration—Not more than 28 days. The patient has right to apply to a Mental Health Review tribunal within first 14 days.

Renewal—By application under Section 3 (Admission for Treatment).

Section 4: Admission for assessment in case of emergency

Applicant—(i) Nearest relative; or (ii) approved social worker.

Medical recommendation—by one medical practitioner, preferably having previous acquaintance with the patient.

Grounds—(i) Admission as under Section 2, is urgently required, and (ii) admission under Section 2 would involve undesirable delay.

Duration—Not more than 72 hours.

Renewal—By means of a second medical recommendation of under Section 2, which is received by the hospital managers within the duration of Section 4. Thus, Section 4 can be converted to Section 2, or Section 3 (Admission for Treatment).

Section 5(2): Application in respect of a patient already in hospital

Section 5(2) allows detention of a patient already receiving any form of inpatient treatment. The application must be made by report from the doctor in charge of the case, or his nominated deputy, if it appears that an application for compulsory detention is warranted as the patient is presenting a danger to himself or others.

Duration of detention under Section 5(2) is for up to 72 hours.

Section 5(4): Nurses' holding power

Section 5(4) allows nurses of a prescribed class (equivalent of a registered mental nurse) to detain a patient, already receiving treatment for mental disorder in hospital, for up to 6 hours while a doctor is found. It must appear to the nurse that (i) the patient is suffering from mental disorder to such a degree that immediate restraint from leaving hospital is necessary for his health or safety, or for the protection of others; and (ii) that it is not practicable to secure the immediate attendance of a practitioner for the purpose of formulating a report under Section 5(2).

5

Brief problem-orientated treatment

It was pointed out in Chapter 4 that most patients who take overdoses or injure themselves do not require psychiatric inpatient care because they are able to take responsibility for themselves or have sufficient support available. Many of these patients will be offered further help of one kind or another. This chapter is primarily concerned with an approach to the care of overdose patients which is brief and focused on helping the patient to solve his own problems. The same principles apply in the management of many patients who injure themselves, but because such patients may also require other forms of help they are dealt with separately in Chapter 8.

Most self-poisoning patients are reacting to crises in interpersonal relationships. Therefore, the treatment approach is based to a large extent on the principles of crisis intervention (Caplan 1964; Brandon 1979; Ewing 1978; Bancroft 1979). The inexperienced therapist often feels that he lacks knowledge of sophisticated treatment techniques. He need not feel this, for crisis intervention is based on relatively simple common-sense principles.

The approach described here was developed on the basis of the experience of an emergency psychiatric service in a general hospital in which both psychiatrists and non-medical staff (nurses and social workers) carry out assessments and treatment (Hawton *et al.* 1979). The principles are equally applicable in many other therapeutic situations, not just those involving patients who have taken overdoses. The approach is particularly likely to be suitable for patients who are seeking help for social and personal problems, and should therefore be useful for many situations encountered by social workers, general practitioners, and those involved in marital counselling, bereavement counselling, and the care of adolescents.

Most overdoses are taken when individuals are finding it difficult to sort out their life problems in a clear way. For this reason, the approach to treatment must, above all else, be a clear one; that is, one which helps the patient separate out each of his problems and plan ways of dealing with them. Some patients want no further contact with the would-be therapist after the initial assessment, or agree to see him only a few times. In most cases, therefore, short-term intervention with realistic goals should be the aim.

They are five stages to management and these are closely interrelated. They are:

1. Assessment of the problems associated with the overdose, of the overdose itself, and of how the problems might be overcome.

2. Problem-solving. The provision of appropriate help to enable the patient himself to resolve the crisis and eventually overcome his problems. This approach can be integrated in conjoint and family therapy as well as as in individual therapy.

3. Preventive measures. To help the patient prevent or cope with subsequent crises without resorting to self-poisoning.

4. Termination.

5. Follow-up.

ASSESSMENT

This was dealt with thoroughly in Chapter 4. It is sufficient to remind the reader here of some of the points pertinent to the form of treatment to be described. First, a rational plan of action can only be arrived at *after the patient's problems have been identified*. Their nature and duration must be defined *precisely*. Careful and accurate description of the problems is necessary before deciding what help is appropriate and what the patient needs to do to overcome his difficulties. The problem list is likely to be most useful if it has been jointly formulated by the patient and the therapist (p. 70).

Secondly, the therapist must be aware of the patient's *coping resources and supportive relationships*. Thus, he should have investigated how the patient has coped previously. This is probably best accomplished by asking the patient to describe difficult situations he has experienced (such as death of a parent, break-up of a relationship, or loss of a job) and the ways in which he managed to resolve them. The therapist must also determine whether the patient feels able, with support, to tackle his present difficulties, and whether another person (such as a partner, confidant, social worker, or general practitioner) is available who might give help now, or to whom the patient could turn if necessary.

Thirdly, a firm plan of subsequent treatment is often only possible when *information* has been gathered from the general practitioner, relatives, friends, and other involved agencies as well as the patient. The plan must depend upon the patient's wish for help and on what is feasible.

Fourthly, from the outset it is important to be sure that there is agreement with the patient about what is planned. The *contract* ideally should include:

1. Which of the patient's problems will be tackled.
2. The type of changes in the problems that will be aimed at.
3. Who else, if anyone, will be involved in treatment and who the therapist will keep informed about the patient's progress.
4. Practical arrangements, including the proposed number of treatment sessions, the likely duration of sessions, their timing and where they will occur. In addition, any arrangement concerning *open access* to the therapist (p. 105) should be discussed.
5. The responsibilities of the patient, such as to attend sessions, to be frank about progress, and to work actively at his problems; and of the therapist, including to keep arrangements made, to listen, to ensure confidentiality, and to help the patient find solutions to his difficulties where possible.

Finally, other people involved in the patient's care should be clear about what is happening. Confusion for both patient and helpers will otherwise result.

PROBLEM-SOLVING

Introduction

In describing the essential ingredients of the problem-orientated approach there is a danger of giving the impression that treatment is usually uncomplicated and straightforward. Unfortunately, in practice this is often not so. Because of the nature of deliberate self-poisoning and the type of individuals involved, some patients may be reluctant to adopt a problem-solving approach to their difficulties, perhaps preferring rapid, if in the long-term unhelpful, solutions, such as dealing with tension by abusing alcohol or drugs, or by making hasty major decisions. However, clinical and research experience has convinced us that if therapists maintain a problem-orientated approach as central to their work this enables them to keep their interventions focused on the most important issues for each patient. Therapists should also be flexible so that they can modify their therapeutic approach according to patients' needs.

Ideally, the aims of this phase of treatment are to help the patient obtain: (i) resolution of the crisis which precipitated the overdose; (ii) alleviation of his social and personal problems; and (iii) a greater ability to cope with similar situations in the future.

The emphasis throughout this approach to treatment is on encouraging the patient to develop the skills to solve his own problems. The therapist helps to set goals and suggests means of attaining them, but tries whenever possible to put responsibility on the patient. Dependence often develops, but need not necessarily be discouraged unless it persists when the patient has managed to overcome most or all of his problems.

Who should be involved in treatment sessions?

If a patient's problems centre on a relationship with a partner or family member(s), and if the relationship is to continue, it is usually essential that these people are included in the treatment sessions. The therapist will otherwise receive a one-sided and often unavoidably distorted view of the relationship, and it is less likely that worthwhile change will be achieved. A case example in which this problem is illustrated is provided later (p. 123). The application of the problem-solving approach in conjoint and family therapy is discussed towards the end of this chapter.

Frequency and duration of treatment sessions

It is usually appropriate to see patients one to three times per week at first; sessions after this can be spaced out to provide continuing support as changes are consolidated. Few patients need help for more than three months; many require only two or three sessions. In a recent study of outpatient counselling of overdose patients, the average number of treatment sessions after the initial assessment was three, with a range of between one and eight sessions (Hawton *et al.* 1987). The frequency of sessions should be determined by the patient's needs and not by a rigid (e.g. weekly) schedule. At the same time it is important not to respond to any minor stress or new problem with an immediate appointment unless really necessary; telephone contact is often a useful alternative. However, if frequent visits are planned, the dangers of dependence on the therapist should be borne in mind.

Treatment sessions do not usually need to be longer than 1 hour. Often 30–40 minutes is enough.

Where should treatment occur?

It is important for hospital-based therapists to realize that many self-poisoning patients fail to keep outpatient appointments. This is not always attributable to 'poor motivation'. It may result from inconveniently timed appointments or travel difficulties; or it may be because the patient lacks clear understanding of what will happen if he does attend.

Treatment at home has advantages for some patients, although it requires more of the therapist's time in travelling. The drop-out rate is far lower, and patients often find it more acceptable. It is easier to involve other family members and useful information may be gained by seeing a patient in his home. It is also more likely that patients, and their partners, will see how treatment is related to their everyday lives, and they will be able to act on the feelings more immediately and carry out the tasks arising from the session. In outpatients, on the other hand, the therapist has more control; at home patients can, if they wish, arrange distractions which make treatment difficult or even impossible.

There is no evidence that home-based treatment results in better outcome than outpatient care (see Chapter 9 and Hawton *et al.* 1981*a*). Nevertheless, if it is doubtful that a patient will keep his first appointment, or if more information about his home circumstances is required, it may be helpful to start therapy at home and continue in outpatients.

A further possibility, where this is available, is to arrange for the patient to attend a psychiatric unit as a day patient. Here treatment can be instigated employing the same sort of principles as used with outpatients. Treatment along similar lines in groups can be a means of making the maximal use of therapists' time (Temple and Catalan 1977). Group treatment can also provide an opportunity for patients to share experiences and learn from each other. The use of groups in the management of self-poisoning patients warrants further investigation.

Patients refusing or dropping out of treatment

Patients sometimes refuse treatment that the therapist thinks potentially helpful. In that case the therapist should reconsider whether he has really offered appropriate help and whether the patient has understood what would be involved; for example, the goals to be pursued and the duration of treatment. If no further contact can be made the general practitioner should be informed. If appropriate, open access may be offered (see p. 105). The same should be done when a patient drops out of treatment, except that, in this case, it is usual to offer another appointment, reiterating the therapist's willingness to help.

Therapist's attitude

This is important in the treatment of self-poisoning patients because, as has already been noted, they are at times regarded with hostility by hospital staff (p. 22), and by relatives and friends (p. 23). It can be extremely helpful if the therapist tells the patient that he is concerned about him, although caution must be exercised not to step outside a professional relationship nor to encourage over-dependency. The patient's self-esteem can be enhanced by reminding him of positive aspects of his personality or previous accomplishments. The therapist should also reward any positive changes by expressing satisfaction and by indicating their potential long-term benefits.

Role of the general practitioner

Treatment plans should be discussed with the patient's general practitioner at an early stage and his views taken into consideration. In many cases it is particularly important to discuss the resons for not prescribing psychotropic drugs. Some general practitioners will prefer to carry out treatment themselves, but may welcome the therapist's advice on management.

Table 11

Brief problem-orientated treatment: the principal components of treatment

---

  1. General approach to problem-solving:
      Identification of problems
      Establishment of goals
      Clarification of steps necessary to achieve goals
      Choice of tasks
      Review progress
      Choice of subsequent tasks
  2. Modification of attitudes
  3. Facilitation of communication
  4. Contracting
  5. Providing information
  6. Advice
  7. Drug prescribing
  8. Referral to other agencies
  9. Preventive measures

THE COMPONENTS OF TREATMENT

The principal components of the problem-solving approach to treatment are summarized in Table 11. Although preventive measures are an intregral part of the approach, and therefore included in the list, they pose particular problems in the management of self-poisoning patients and are therefore considered in a separate section. The Table does not include various non-specific measures which are part of any treatment procedure of this kind. *Listening, providing support, and general encouragement* are the most important of these.

General approach to problem-solving

Central to problem-solving is a general approach in which the therapist tries to help the patient draw on his own resources to overcome his problems. The principles that the therapist and patient should adhere to are as follows.

Define the problem(s) to be tackled

Problems can be divided into those requiring a *choice between alternatives* (e.g. shall I take this job; shall I leave my spouse?) and those requiring the *attainment of specific goals* (e.g. how can I do my job better; how can I improve the relationship with my spouse?). Sometimes this stage is straightforward because the problems are obvious (e.g. inability to pay a debt; a specific sexual dysfunction). Very often it demands considerable time and careful exploration to help the patient decide precisely what his problems are. This is more likely when, for example, the difficulties concern the general aspects of a relationship, or non-specific dissatisfaction a person may experience with his current lifestyle.

Establish suitable clear goals

The goals should be *realistic* (i.e. attainable in a relatively short time) and *specific*. This stage can also sometimes be straightforward. Thus, a reasonable goal related to a problem of boredom in an adolescent because of lack of interests might be to join a local youth club. However, selection of goals often can be extremely difficult. The therapist can usually help by suggesting a series of possibilities and then having the patient consider each in turn. The patient's engagement in such exploration may sometimes be facilitated by including a clearly inappropriate possibility that he can easily reject. He may then find it easier to start considering more likely possibilities.

Clarify the steps necessary to obtain these goals and the likely consequences

In doing so, the therapist should help the patient consider all reasonable alternatives. It is often worthwhile looking at methods the patient has previously tried to use for the present problem to see whether, with modification, these might be tried again. In addition, successful methods employed in the past to solve other problems should be investigated. It is most important that the patient considers the likely consequences of different ways of trying to achieve goals. By this means the most appropriate course of action often becomes apparent. For example, a man who wished to make certain grievances clear to his boss decided that this was best approached, in the first instance, by writing to his boss because he realized that, were he to try to do this face to face, he would find it difficult to express himself without losing his temper.

At this stage, the patient often sees more clearly the appropriate course of action, whereas previously he was in a turmoil of indecision.

Agree what the patient has to do before the next session

The steps should be chosen primarily by the patient; the therapist should discuss ways of carrying them out. It is important that the tasks agreed upon are absolutely clear. This make misunderstandings, as well as evasion, less likely. Examples of such tasks are: an adolescent girl who has been having unprotected sexual intercourse with her boyfriend agrees to go to her local family planning clinic to seek contraceptive advice and to avoid having intercourse until contraception has been arranged; a student with difficulty getting down to revising for an important examination decides that he must make a list of what he needs to do—his therapist suggests he also arranges the topics in their order of importance.

Quite often a patient remains undecided at this stage about which goal to pursue. This often applies where a patient is faced by alternative choices. In such circumstances a useful task can be for the patient to draw up a list of pros and cons of the two alternatives. This is likely to facilitate subsequent decision-making and can provide useful material for discussion at the next session.

Review progress in detail

At the next session, after enquiring about the patient's well-being, the therapist should clarify precisely what happened when the patient attempted his task(s). Appropriate praise and encouragement should be offered for any progress the patient has made. This is likely to be most important early in therapy when his self-confidence may be low. If the patient has successfully carried out the task that was agreed he should now be helped to plan what to do before the next session. Thus, for example, the student with difficulty revising, having drawn up his plan of action, agreed to work on the first item on his list and not to be side-tracked into attempting other items at the same time.

When a patient has failed to do what had been agreed the therapist must encourage him to explore in detail the reasons for this. The therapist should in particular look for, and assist the patient to recognize, attitudes which have prevented the achievement of tasks. Ways of helping patients modify their attitudes are discussed below.

Sometimes a patient will have failed to carry out his task because it was inappropriate or too demanding. Then the therapist needs to help him explore alternative approaches to the problem, or find some way of breaking the task down into more manageable steps.

Modification of attitudes

It has already been noted that obstructive attitudes can prevent progress in therapy, and that such attitudes can usually be identified by carefully analysing the patient's attempts to achieve goals and the reason for failure. Helping the patient to modify such attitudes may sometimes be necessary before he is able to change his behaviour or effectively pursue tasks necessary to achieve his chosen goals. This is usually the most difficult part of treatment.

Attitudes which are often encountered include those associated with *low self-esteem* (e.g. 'It's no use trying because everything I attempt fails', or 'I don't deserve to succeed'). Sometimes such attitudes are secondary to a patient's current mood state; in other cases they are long-standing and firmly established. If the latter then considerable difficulty may be encountered in trying to help the patient change his attitudes. Probably the most effective means is to find a task which is sufficiently simple that the patient can carry it out and thereby begin to experience success. Another approach which is complementary to this is to encourage the patient to examine the questions and assumptions that prevent him getting started on anything.

There are two further approaches to modifying attitudes. The first is *confrontation*. Thus, it may be desirable to draw a patient's attention to any inconsistency between his expressed attitudes and his actual behaviour (e.g. a therapist pointed out to a patient that the latter insisted that he wished to tackle some problem in his home yet arranged to go out every evening with his friends). The second is *interpretation*. This is difficult to define satisfactorily, but in the context of brief therapy it involves the therapist suggesting to the patient the possible motivation underlying his behaviour, with the objective of increasing understanding as a step towards behaviour change (e.g. overeating may be explained in terms of a patient's need for comfort at times of loneliness so that the patient may be more able to tackle the problem). The patient should be encouraged to try to find a suitable explanation first, before the therapist considers providing one of his own.

In order to get a patient actively involved in considering explanations for his behaviour it can be useful to offer him several possibilities to examine, especially if these include one or two explanations which are clearly unlikely and which he can easily refute.

Facilitation of communication

Many overdose patients are unable to discuss their needs and emotions with their partners or families. The resulting frustration may be, in part, why they have taken an overdose. Improvement in communication is therefore an important goal.

Communication problems may occur in the *exchange of information* and the *expression of emotion*. Joint sessions with the partner or close relatives are often the best means of dealing with these problems. Faulty communication patterns can be directly pointed out, and steps towards improving them can then be recommended.

Examples of emotions that may need to be expressed are:

1. *Grief*, where loss has occurred, either through death or separation. Because of cultural, family or personality factors many people may suppress their grief, but allowing grief to be expressed often reduces its intensity or duration.

2. *Anger*, which may not be expressed because of personality factors, such as excessive control, or fear of the consequences. In a continuing relationship the expression of anger sometimes needs to be encouraged by the therapist to allow the partners to improve other aspects of their relationship. If anger follows the break-up of a relationship, the therapist may encourage its expression and explain that it is a normal and healthy reaction.

Contracting

The patient may improve his chances of achieving a goal by entering into a contract with himself or someone else. Thus in a *self-contract* he may make a contract such as 'if at the end of the week I have gone without a drink, or lost x lbs in weight, I can buy myself . . .'. In a *couple or family contract* the patient and his partner, for example, may undertake to do things on a reciprocal basis (e.g. a husband agrees to organize weekly social outings for he and his wife, while she agrees to tell him when she is feeling distressed, rather than keeping her feelings to herself). However, couple contracts are more likely to succeed if they are not directly reciprocal. Thus, the partners should decide what each needs to do to improve the relationship and then attempt to make these changes, without the behaviour of one being entirely contingent on whether or not the other partner does what was agreed.

Contracting may be effective because it makes evasion difficult, facilitates communication, and offers rewards to the patient. The therapist's role is to instigate contracts and to encourage their implementation [see Chapter 8 of Stuart (1980) for further details of contractual therapy with couples].

Providing information

A therapist will often need to provide patients with information on the basis of his professional knowledge (e.g. explaining the side-effects of psychotropic medication). This is usually done in order to reassure the patient (e.g. explaining that it is customary for a person's interest in sex to be impaired when depressed). It is also quite common for a therapist to provide information in order to correct misinformed beliefs (e.g. a patient was allowing an early, unwanted pregnancy to proceed because she thought that abortion was likely to make a woman sterile).

Advice

Although a therapist should avoid being too directive, as this is likely to encourage dependency and may discourage a patient from developing his coping skills, it is quite often appropriate to offer advice. Thus he might suggest that a patient makes contact with a helping agency (e.g. a Family Planning Clinic, Citizens' Advice Bureau, Cruse, Shelter, Friend, Gay Switchboard). He may need to advise how to obtain legal help or financial guidance. Advice on the use of money may also occasionally be necessary.

Drug prescribing

In the management of self-poisoning patients being considered here, it is seldom necessary to introduce psychotropic drugs. Indeed, more often it is necessary to consider stopping psychotropic drugs already prescribed. Such drugs often have been inappropriately prescribed and also have been used in the overdose (p. 40).

Psychotropic drugs should only be prescribed for good reasons. For example, if there is evidence of significant depression which is severely limiting coping ability. When antidepressants are prescribed, the therapist's role is largely to provide support until the patient's mood improves sufficiently for him to tackle his problems himself. Problems in personal relationships are unlikely to be altered directly by medication. However, if such problems are secondary to a mood disturbance in one or other partner, considerable improvement may occur after the introduction of appropriate medication.

A patient may be so anxious that he cannot begin to act in a way which would resolve his problems. A tranquillizer may help to reduce anxiety so that the person is better able to start tackling his problems, but the drug should only be used for a short time (up to 2 weeks), and should be withdrawn once improvement in coping ability has begun to develop. There are, however, very few indications for tranquillizers in people who are experiencing personal and interpersonal problems. Brief counselling is at least as effective as medication in most people facing such problems (Catalan *et al.* 1984a).

Insomnia may profoundly impair coping and need treatment in its own right. If hypnotics are prescribed, enough tablets for only a few nights should be given at any one time and the medication stopped once the period of distress is over. The reason for prescribing this medication, and the plan for its use should be explained to the patient and agreed upon before a prescription is supplied.

Good collaboration between non-medical therapists and their medical colleagues should mean that the former can suggest the introduction or withdrawal of medication. However, definitive decisions about such measures must rest with medically qualified personnel.

Referral to other agencies

It may help to refer the patient to other agencies (e.g. social services, a psychosexual problems clinic, self-help groups). These agencies can offer forms of help that usually cannot be provided by the therapist (e.g. obtaining rehousing, meeting other people with similar interests). The patient may be referred to such agencies either during or at the end of treatment.

A small minority of overdose patients have psychological difficulties for which a problem-solving approach will be insufficient, except in helping resolve the current crisis. These include individuals with long-standing problems of low self-esteem, especially when these have their origins in unsatisfactory or unhappy experiences during their early development. In such cases some form of longer-term individual or group psychotherapy may be beneficial, although the therapist must be convinced that the patient has sufficient motivation and ability to explore psychological phenomena before making a referral for psychotherapy. A brief period of problem-orientated counselling will often help clarify whether such a referral is appropriate. Similarly, patients with long-standing depression or chronic anxiety, including those with panic attacks, may be helped by cognitive therapy (Beck *et al.* 1979; Beck and Emery 1984). This approach, while including elements of problem-solving, focuses particularly on the thinking style and negative self-ideas that perpetuate affective disorders.

Setting limits to treatment

Patients sometimes make demands on a therapist which exceed what can reasonably be expected of a therapeutic relationship and which do not appear likely to help solve their problems. When a therapist becomes aware that such a situation is developing it is most important that he discusses this with the patient and sets very clear limits on the relationship. The following case summary illustrates a situation where this was necessary.

Janet, a 14-year-old schoolgirl, had taken an overdose of paracetamol in circumstances which suggested low suicidal intent. At first the therapist was not clear what Janet's problems were, despite interviewing her parents and her year tutor at school. However, when seen again as an outpatient 2 days later, she admitted the overdose had been related to feeling rejected by a master at school with whom she was infatuated. She was now fearful about returning to school, but agreed to discuss this with her tutor. Over the next 2 weeks she telephoned the therapist two or three times a week complaining of a variety of physical symptoms and demanding to be seen straight away. In addition she had made suicide threats to a friend, who also telephoned the therapist.

During the next two sessions, Janet revealed several difficulties in her relationship with her parents. Despite some improvements having occurred in her problems, she continued telephoning the therapist, making threats of suicide and demanding to be seen. The therapist regarded this behaviour as resulting from Janet's dependence on her and fear of losing her support. This was discussed at length with Janet, after which it was agreed that the therapist would see her for the next 2 months at fortnightly intervals and that no more than one telephone call per week would be acceptable. The arrangement was also discussed with her parents. It was made clear that if Janet were to break this agreement the therapist would discontinue contact with her.

Janet tested the therapist's determination during the first week by threatening to take an overdose if a second telephone call was not accepted. Thereafter, she complied with the arrangement. In addition, she stopped acting out, both at home and at school, and the therapy sessions became more productive.

Working with couples and with families

In view of how often overdoses result from relationship problems it is not surprising that the most effective treatment of self-poisoners often occurs in conjoint therapy with the partner or in family therapy. In either of these approaches, problem-solving should be a major element. When working with couples, the therapist's role is to help the partners identify the problems that they face as a couple and then to encourage them to tackle those that appear soluble using the approach that has already been described. Contracting (p. 98) is a useful core-element in conjoint work. Particular attention should be paid to facilitating communication between the partners, especially in the treatment sessions. The presence of the therapist can encourage partners to express their anxieties, needs, and wishes to each other, whereas previously they may have found this extremely difficult or even impossible. Discussion of each individual's understanding of the overdose can be a potent means of initiating such communication, as well as allowing expression of feelings about the act (p. 23). Clearly, the therapist must avoid taking sides in such discussion.

Family therapy will be of most use with young self-poisoners (Richman 1979), although occasionally it can be appropriate with adult attempters, especially if the attempt has brought to light disturbed family dynamics and other family members are willing to participate in treatment. The principal aims of family therapy are usually: (i) the modification of interactions, especially communication patterns, between family members; (ii) fostering support between family members; and (iii) improving the family's problem-solving behaviour.

As with other therapeutic approaches, family therapy includes several phases. In the first phase the therapist will be assessing the structure of the family, current communication patterns, how family members either support or undermine each other, and the ability of the family to address problems. It is always necessary for the therapist to emphasize the strengths as well as the weakness of individual family members and of the family as a whole. The therapeutic contract will be of utmost importance, and will include the specific goals of therapy, who will attend treatment sessions, and how many sessions will be involved. A limited contract for a few sessions, at least in the first instance, is always preferable.

Encouraging the family to discuss a particular current issue that it is facing is often the best way of assessing the factors noted above. Once the therapist is confident of his assessment he can point out ways in which communication might be improved or how family members can support each other more. The aim will then be to encourage the family to try and modify their interactions within the therapy session, before practising this at home. Similarly, the therapist should help the family formulate a step-by-step approach to problem-solving with regard to a particular problem, and then encourage them to try out these steps at home, reporting back at subsequent sessions on their progress and any difficulties that they have encountered.

A crucial element in family therapy involves encouraging the autonomy of family members in working out their own solutions to problems and taking responsibility for their own actions, the therapist acting largely as an independent facilitator. Avoidance of unwittingly taking-sides with individual members is essential.

While this approach might appear to be the treatment of choice for many adolescent self-poisoners, in practice, family therapy is often difficult to establish because of the reluctance of some family members to become involved. Sometimes this is because of fear of 'psychiatric' treatment (Taylor and Stansfield 1984). Often, however, this reluctance appears to reflect the severity of the disturbance in the family.

PREVENTIVE MEASURES

Treatment should include preparing the patient, couple, or family for future crises. Implicit in the use of the problem-solving approach described above is the aim of helping people acquire coping skills which can be used not just to solve the current problems but also to deal with some of those that may occur subsequently. However, there are special difficulties inherent in treating overdose patients. The first is that the act of self-poisoning may have been rewarding in so far as any subsequent positive changes could be seen as resulting from the act itself. Secondly, as previously discussed (p. 40), self-poisoning is often impulsive, and it is difficult to devise ways of combating this impulsivity.

Despite these difficulties it is essential that the therapist should try to incorporate preventive measures in his treatment. The following are strategies which can be employed.

The reasons for the overdose should be discussed with both the patient and his partner or family. The aim is to enable the patient to understand the effects of his behaviour on other people and at the same time to help others understand their role in the behaviour. It is often better to leave such exploration until the patient's difficulties are beginning to resolve because by then the patient may be more willing to consider, for example, that his act was based on hostile and manipulation motives. However, the ventilation of feelings about the overdose, especially those experienced by the partner or other family members, should be encouraged early in therapy, otherwise they may impede progress.

Open discussion of self-poisoning as a method of coping. The therapist should indicate other less disruptive methods of obtaining help and bringing about change. However, these methods must have some appeal to the patient. Such measures become all the more important when the overdose is a repeat.

Presenting the patient with hypothetical, but realistic crisis-provoking situations similar to those which he has experienced and then examining in detail other ways of dealing with them apart from self-poisoning. The patient might rehearse in imagination the most constructive alternative so that he may readily adopt it if a crisis occurs. The patient's partner should be involved in such discussion, if appropriate, but particularly if the main problems that led to referral centre on this relationship.

Open access by telephone to an emergency service may be offered if such a facility exists locally. This might be based on a psychiatric clinic or a voluntary agency such as the Samaritans. Some patients are helped by knowing this is available although they may never use it. In each case the therapist should discuss how to make use of the open access facility. Depending on his assessment of the patient, the therapist may judge that he should be encouraged to use open access only as a last resort; in other cases it has to be accepted that the patient and his relatives may benefit if they can use this facility often. The following example illustrates how open access can be used.

Mary, a 26-year-old woman with two children aged 1 and 3, had divorced her husband 6 months before her overdose and gone back to live with her parents. Two months later her gall bladder had been removed, but she continued to experience abdominal discomfort. Three months later she left her parents and went to live with her boyfriend Peter. She took her overdose after a row with him. Mary would not allow Peter to be involved in treatment. However, she agreed to see the therapist as an outpatient, and to use open access by telephone if in the meantime she felt unable to cope with her difficulties. After keeping the first appointment she failed to attend two further treatment sessions, telephoning the therapist after the second to say she felt better. However, the therapist did not think that the situation had improved and therefore offered further open access.

Mary telephoned the therapist 2 months later because she felt unable to decide whether to return to her ex-husband or to stay with her boyfriend. She attended another treatment session to discuss her difficulties further. However, she said she would now prefer to try to cope without coming to the hospital but would appreciate being able to telephone the therapist if necessary. She also said she was sure she would not take a further overdose. She contacted the therapist on two occasions because of continuing uncertainty about which relationship to pursue. The therapist thought Mary appeared to benefit from these telephone contacts and had not abused the availability of open access.

The chronic repeater

Patients who repeatedly take overdoses pose considerable management difficulties. The problem-orientated approach is not usually effective with such patients. When a patient seems to be developing a pattern of chronic repeats, it is recommended that all staff engaged in his or her care meet to reconstruct each attempt in order to determine whether there appears to be a motive common to each act. A patient for whom such a motive was found was described earlier (p. 19). If this is the case then the motivational aspects of the behaviour should be discussed further with the patient in order to explore alternative means of achieving the objective of the attempts. However, the impulsive nature of such repeats, which is often related to alcohol abuse, can make alternative measures, which appear practical to the therapist, totally inappropriate for the patient. In this case the treatment team may have to accept that the best it can offer is long-term support and encouragement, with treatment sessions being non-contingent on repeats. If a repeat does occur the immediate response should be a brief interview sufficient to make a satisfactory assessment, especially with regard to suicidal intent. Repetition with increasing suicidal intent can be a forewarning that the patient is likely to make a fatal attempt (Pierce 1981). Brief admission for psychiatric impatient care may then be indicated.

TERMINATION

The end of treatment must be planned from the start. The therapist should prepare the patient for termination by making it clear from the first interview that a relatively short period of treatment is planned. Nevertheless, the therapist should always deal with termination by finding out how the patient feels about treatment coming to an end. Some patients will be relieved because of the independence and sense of accomplishment that termination brings. Others may be fearful that they will not be able to cope without the support and guidance of the therapist. Such patients may be helped by being reminded of what they have accomplished during treatment. As discussed earlier (p. 101), a patient thought to require further or more prolonged help may be referred for another kind of treatment.

The patient's general practitioner should be informed that treatment is ending. He may also welcome advice on how he might continue the therapeutic process and deal with any further crises.

FOLLOW-UP

Termination of treatment may be facilitated by the patient, couple, or family being offered a follow-up appointment 1–2 months later. Apart from providing a sense of continuing support, a follow-up interview allows the therapist to assess the progress since the end of treatment, and offer praise and encouragement if appropriate. It also provides an opportunity for the therapist to re-evaluate the need for either additional or alternative treatment. Finally, it enables the therapist to assess the effectiveness of his own clinical skills and, hopefully, to improve them in future.

CONCLUSIONS

In this chapter a therapeutic approach that can be used with a large proportion of patients who take overdoses has been described. It does not require a great deal of specialist training other than in counselling skills and is based on common sense. Apart from its use with attempted suicide patients it is readily applicable to many other situations where patients require help with social or personal problems, and can be integrated into conjoint and family therapy, as well as in the treatment of individuals. The approach is primarily focused on helping patients resolve the crisis that has led to an overdose and on tackling their longer-term problems, largely using their own resources to do so and thereby developing greater ability to cope with stresses in future. Regular supervision meetings with an experienced therapist, or case demonstrations, can assist therapists to develop their skills in the application of this problem-orientated approach. In the next chapter the treatment approach is illustrated by a description of cases in which it was used.

6

Examples of brief treatment of overdose patients

This chapter is devoted to the description of clinical cases in order to illustrate the practical use of the techniques of assessment and brief problem-orientated treatment that were described in Chapters 4 and 5. Similar principles were applied to the assessment of each case. First, the circumstances surrounding the overdose were elucidated and the patient's mental state assessed. Other people who could provide corroborative or extra information were interviewed. In each case a detailed problem list was establish, and the therapist also tried to understand the reasons for the behaviour. The final stage of assessment was the negotiation of a treatment contract, including which of the patient's problems were going to be tackled and the practical arrangements for treatment sessions.

In describing subsequent treatment, the contents of each treatment session are summarized. The aim is to illustrate the feasibility of a brief and practical approach to treatment based largely on common sense. Examples are provided of the use of medication, including stopping such treatment when it does not appear to be helping a patient. The importance of collaborating with the patient's general practitioner is emphasized. In some of the cases new problems, not identified at the outset, emerged during the course of treatment. The use of preventive measures is also illustrated.

The five cases have been chosen to provide examples of different types of problems commonly found among self-poisoning patients, all of which may be tackled using a brief treatment approach with problem-solving as its central theme. The first and third cases both involve individuals who had recently experienced the break-up of a relationship with a partner. In these examples the therapists endeavoured to help the patients come to terms with the loss and at the same time tried to assist them to tackle the other problems they were facing. The second case provides an example of a disturbed marital relationship where the therapist helped the partners work together to solve their problems. The fourth case, apart from illustrating the typical problems of an adolescent self-poisoner, is also included as an example of treatment which did not have a very good outcome, probably because the therapist did not involve the patient's parents from an early stage. The final case, which illustrates the difficulties that unemployed attempters often face, also provides a typical example of the use of brief problem-orientated treatment.

All five cases are based on actual patients. However, as elsewhere in this book, details of each case, including the patients' names, have been modified in order to ensure anonymity.

CASE I—AN IMPULSIVE OVERDOSE

This first example illustrates an impulsive overdose taken by a woman who had experienced a recent loss and had been unable to discuss her problems with her family. During the relatively short treatment, the therapist helped the patient to begin discussing her feelings with her family. Time was also spent exploring the consequences of the overdose and finding alternative ways of coping with similar problems in the future.

Background

Liz, a 25-year-old single woman, had been living on her own for the previous year in a flat above a small craft shop that she ran together with her mother. During this time, Liz had taken much of the responsibility for the day-to-day running of the business, while her mother had been staying at home to look after her husband who was in poor health. Six months before her overdose Liz terminated the relationship with her boyfriend of two years' standing after she discovered he had been going out with another girl. Since then she had tended to spend more time on her own in the flat and to stay with her parents at weekends. At the same time she had become less interested in the shop and was failing to keep the books and correspondence in order.

Circumstances of the overdose

Liz had spent the weekend with her parents as usual. On Sunday all of them had attended a cousin's wedding. Late that evening Liz returned to her flat, where she felt lonely and miserable, particularly when she remembered how happy everyone had seemed earlier in the day. When she went to bed she found it impossible to sleep, and started thinking about her ex-boyfriend and about the paperwork that awaited her the next day. Just before midnight she got up and swallowed two aspirins with some water which she hoped would calm her down. After a few minutes she decided to take another two tables and then continued taking two at a time until she had swallowed about 30. Forty tablets remained in the bottle. She then went to bed feeling more relaxed, but after a while felt unwell and was soon sick. This happened several times during the night. At 6.00 a.m. Liz telephoned her parents and told them she had been sick, but did not mention the overdose. About an hour later her mother arrived and, when Liz explained what she had done, telephoned for an ambulance.

Assessment

When the therapist interviewed her later on the same day, Liz felt very embarrassed about the overdose and about being in hospital. She said she had not wanted to die but that she had taken the tablets to calm herself down in order to get some sleep. She was able to give a good account of herself and was reasonably cheerful during the interview, except when she talked about her boyfriend and about the distress she had caused her parents. Her suicidal intent as measured by the Beck Suicidal Intent Scale was low (total score = 3).

Liz was prepared to allow the therapist to talk to her parents, but she did not want her to tell them about her problems concerning the shop, preferring to discuss these with them herself. The therapist thought the overdose was not a serious suicidal attempt but appeared to be an impulsive act to escape from her feelings of loneliness and worry about the shop. There was no evidence of her having a psychiatric disorder, although it was clear that she had become somewhat withdrawn and had lost confidence in herself since the break-up of her relationship with her boyfriend.

Liz's parents were interviewed by the therapist. They were an elderly and well-meaning couple who appeared very protective towards her. They were worried about her being alone in the flat and had wondered whether she was pregnant or had taken drugs.

Initial problem list

The following problem list was compiled by Liz together with her therapist:

1. Problems coping with the shop, particularly in dealing with bills and accounts (for the last 6 months).

2. Difficulty accepting the break-up of the relationship with her boyfriend (for the past 6 months, worse in the last day).

3. Inability to discuss problems 1 and 2 with her parents (for the last 6 months).

4. Social isolation (for the last 6 months).

5. Loss of confidence in herself: (i) self-blame concerning break-up of relationship; (ii) unsure about ability to establish another relationship; (iii) feelings of having let her parents down (6 months).

Initial contract

Liz and her therapist arranged to meet initially three times and then decide whether further contact was necessary. Liz felt the main problem was finding a way to talk to her parents about her difficulties with the shop. She wanted to do this on her own and the therapist suggested that the first session took place 2 days later to assess her progress. The therapist discusses these plans with Liz's general practitioner, who was in agreement with the arrangements made.

Treatment

Session one

Liz came back accompanied by her parents, but wanting to speak to the therapist on her own first. She explained that she had not been able to bring herself to discuss things with them, although she had managed to speak to her married brother, who had been very supportive and helpful. Her parents were still concerned about her and she had asked them to accompany her for this first appointment. Liz asked the therapist to talk to her parents on her behalf, but the therapist suggested she herself did it with the therapist's support. A joint meeting followed where Liz discussed her difficulties with her parents. They had already suspected what the problems were, and Liz and her parents soon started to discuss ways in which they could deal with the backlog of paperwork. It was agreed that Liz would talk to her brother again and make use of his advice.

Session two

A week later Liz appeared much more cheerful and explained how she was now catching up with her work. She had been thinking about her future and discussing it with her parents, and all of them had decided to sell the shop. Liz had continued to live at home with her parents, but she was now thinking about going to stay with her brother and his wife for a few weeks.

The therapist pointed out to Liz that she seemed to be trying to get away from both the shop and the flat, and Liz then talked about her life with her boyfriend and that she felt she needed to start afresh. At this point she burst into tears and blamed herself for the break-up of their relationship. Her feelings about it were discussed and in particular her sense of failure and bitterness towards him. The therapist encouraged her to look at herself in a more realistic way, and particularly to try to identify her good points and qualities. The therapist also raised the problem of Liz's social isolation, and together they explored ways of re-establishing her social life. Liz agreed to contact some old friends that she had not seen since before the break-up of the relationship with her boyfriend.

Session three

Two weeks later Liz had moved in with her brother and sister-in-law and seemed much happier in herself. She had re-established contact with her friends and had been out on one occasion in the previous week. She was able to talk about herself in a more positive way, and this she attributed to having felt useful and capable when helping her sister-in-law around the house. On one occasion Liz had felt miserable while thinking about her ex-boyfriend, but she had spoken to her sister-in-law and soon felt much better. She continued to go to the shop and had managed to clear the backlog of work and correspondence.

The possibility of further meetings was discussed and it was agreed to have one more session in a month's time in order to evaluate progress.

Session four

Liz came back looking happier and more confident. She said that people had commented on how she seemed to be back to her usual self, and that things seemed to be going very well with her brother and sister-in-law. She had started to look for another job, as it seemed that it would be possible to sell the shop within the next few weeks. Her social life seemed to be quite full, and she had gone out with a young man on a couple of occasions. Although Liz did not feel this was a serious relationship, she felt more confident about the future and about her ability to form other relationships.

The therapist directed the conversation back to the overdose and its effects. It was clear that things had improved considerably in recent weeks and that this could be seen as a consequence of her having taken the tablets. The therapist pointed out that the changes that had taken place in her life were the result of her having discussed her problems with her family and having taken the necessary steps to solve them. Liz was asked to imagine how she would respond if she was faced with the same problems again. Liz suggested the following ways of dealing with her problems.

1. Doing something about it early when the problems began to develop, rather than later, when they had become fully established.

2. Talking to someone about how she was feeling and not bottling up her worries.

3. Making sure that she remained in contact with people and not socially isolated.

No further appointment was made, but Liz was offered open telephone access to the psychiatric unit in the event of future difficulties.

Summary

This example illustrates how the therapist helped the patient take an active part in clarifying her problems and finding means of solving them. One important objective of counselling was to improve communication within the family, which was achieved in the first session when the therapist took a supportive but firm approach and encouraged the patient to talk to her parents then. At the end of treatment the therapist thought that Liz would probably experience further problems in the future and so discussed with her possible ways of dealing with new difficulties.

CASE II—CHRONIC MARITAL PROBLEMS

This case illustrates the management of a patient who had taken an overdose in the setting of long-standing marital difficulties, and where there were added problems concerning a child. The importance of fully involving the patient's partner in assessment and subsequent treatment is very clear. A problem-solving approach was employed which included the use of contracts to enable the couple to reciprocate efforts at improving their relationship.

Background

Charles, aged 45, had become increasingly frustrated about the deterioration in his relationship with his wife Ann. Both had been having affairs and there had been several brief separations. Despite Charles's own affairs, he could not tolerate his wife seeing other men. He had been violent towards Ann on several occasions. She had a poor relationship with Susan, Charles's 14-year-old daughter from his previous marriage.

Circumstances of the overdose

On the day of the overdose Charles and Ann had a row before he went to work, and later Charles came home to find his wife had left him. He was able to find her and bring her back home where he pleaded with her to stay. When she refused he took an overdose of his barbiturate tablets in front of her. She tried to ignore what he had done. However, when he later became drowsy she telephoned for an ambulance to take him to hospital.

Assessment

Upon recovery from the overdose, Charles said he had not cared whether he lived or died at the time of taking the tablets, but wanted to show Ann how desperate he was feeling. His score on the Beck Suicidal Intent Scale was 4 (this suggests low intent).

During the assessment Ann was interviewed. She made it clear that she wished their relationship to continue, but could not tolerate Charles's violent outbursts. She also felt very angry with him for having taken an overdose.

The therapist did not think Charles was depressed nor suffering from any other psychiatric disorder. There appeared no reason to suspect suicidal intent; rather, the therapist understood the overdose as being intended to evoke sympathy from Ann, to make her feel guilty about leaving home and to put pressure on her to return.

Initial problem list

1. Charles's violent behaviour towards Ann (6 years).
2. Mutual jealousy, particularly concerning affairs they had both held in the past (4 years).
3. Very little social life together (6 years).
4. Charles's receiving barbiturate medication (unnecessarily) for insomnia (9 months).
5. Unsuitable accommodation—a small caravan (6 years).

Charles and Ann agreed with the therapist that this was a reasonable summary of their difficulties.

Initial contract

The therapist arranged with the couple that they would attend between four and six conjoint sessions as outpatients during the next 3–4 weeks in order to explore ways of improving their relationship, particularly their lack of social life together, and of helping Charles control his physical aggression.

Immediately after the assessment interview the therapist telephoned their general practitioner, and informed him of his assessment and proposed management. The general practitioner agreed both to discontinue prescribing Charles's barbiturates and not to give him any further medication.

Treatment

The therapist realized that some changes in the couples' situation would have to occur within a few days if another crisis were to be avoided. The approach he adopted was intended to produce practical changes as soon as possible.

Session one

This took place 4 days after Charles had been discharged from hospital. A Salvation Army officer friend had arranged for Ann to spend a few days away from home to help her resolve her feelings about the crisis before starting to tackle the difficulties in her marriage. Since her return the couple have felt more positive about their relationship and no violent behaviour had occurred. After a couple of nights when he had difficulty in getting to sleep, Charles had slept well.

During this session further exploration of their difficulties had led to the identification of two additional problems:

6. Ann's continuing need for attention and reassurance (4 years).

7. Her frequent thoughts of self-poisoning and the risk of her taking an overdose (3 months). She had taken an overdose 8 years previously.

After the therapist encouraged the couple to think of ways of being positive in their behaviour towards each other, Ann agreed to wear more attractive clothes, and Charles to show her more consideration and affection by praising her appearance, and expressing positive feelings towards her. Thus, the couple had agreed upon a simple contract. The therapist helped them to agree to carry out mutual tasks which were that they would spend one day out together during the next weekend and visit a friend together on another day during the week.

Ann had been taking an antidepressant for 6 months without much benefit. In addition there was a small risk of her taking an overdose. Therefore, the therapist suggested she should stop this medication. He then discussed this with the general practitioner and gradual reduction of the antidepressant was initiated.

Session two

No aggression had occurred since the previous session a week earlier. The couple had carried out all their agreed tasks and Ann had begun to reduce her medication.

In this session Ann talked of her deprived early life and her first marriage, which ended when her husband walked out. She accepted the therapist's simple interpretation that this probably in part explained her excessive need for attention and reassurance from Charles.

The couple agreed on a further weekend outing together. Charles was to play tennis with Ann and she was to let him know when she was feeling upset. She also agreed to tell him each evening about the sort of day she had had while he was at work. The therapist hoped this would further improve their ease of communication. Ann was to stop her medication completely.

Session three

Charles and Ann had been out several times together, there had been no aggression, and they were being more affectionate. Ann had met an old boyfriend, and she and Charles had been able to discuss their feelings about this without animosity. She had stopped her antidepressant. Their therapist expressed his satisfaction with their progress, and pointed out how their efforts were leading to a more rewarding relationship and a general sense of well-being for both of them.

The couple agreed to continue going out socially together, and the therapist agreed to write to the local housing department to back up their application for council accommodation.

Session four

The couple were now enjoying a regular social life together, which included going to the cinema, walking, and visiting friends. However, there was still some unresolved mistrust on both sides. They agreed to continue their efforts to improve their social life and to discuss openly any disagreements or suspicions which cropped up.

Session five

The housing department had approved their application for council accommodation. The goals of the previous session had been achieved. Ann was less demanding and feeling less suspicious of Charles. The couple were helped to explore constructive methods of dealing with future crises without resorting to self-poisoning. They agreed to try to express any feelings of animosity at an early stage, rather than harbouring them until they exploded. They also promised to use their friends in the Salvation Army as supports at times when they thought they could not cope by themselves. A further problem was identified.

8. Ann's intolerant and excessively strict treatment of Charles's daughter Susan (4 years).

Ann was helped to see that this problem originally resulted from displaced resentments about Charles's infidelity. She was then able to suggest ways she might improve this relationship.

Session six

When seen for their final treatment session, 7 weeks after the overdose, the couple's improved social life had been maintained. Ann had been able to show more tolerance towards Susan. Charles and Ann had freely discussed their feelings about each other. Treatment was terminated and open access to the therapist by telephone offered in case they were unable to cope with future crises.

They made contact with the therapist 3 months later when they were unable to resolve a disagreement. They were seen for one further session during which it was possible to help them reach a suitable compromise.

Summary

The importance of looking for reasons to explain aggression or demanding behaviour is well illustrated in this case. Once Ann had been helped to understand that she felt insecure in her relationship with Charles as a result of earlier experiences, she and Charles were then able to commit themselves to a contractual approach to problem-solving. The necessity for assessing the usefulness of psychotropic medication after self-poisoning was apparent for both partners in this case. For neither of them did the medication appear to have been helpful and, in collaboration with their general practitioner, it was therefore stopped. Finally, the importance of sometimes involving other people who can provide support was well illustrated by the role of the Salvation Army friends.

CASE III—MARITAL BREAKDOWN

In contrast to the management of a couple with problems in their relationship, different therapeutic needs are posed by the patient who has suffered the break-up of a relationship. The patient described here took an overdose not long after her marriage somewhat unexpectedly came to an end. The therapist's main task was to help the patient grieve over her loss and adapt to living without a partner. In doing so he also had to try to relieve her symptoms of depression and help her gain control over her alcohol intake.

Background

Margaret was aged 44. She had been married for 19 years and had four children (aged between 12 and 17 years). She had been working full time in a local factory for the past 8 years and usually enjoyed good relationships with her friends. In Margaret's opinion the marriage had been moderately happy until 3 weeks before the overdose when her husband suddenly left home and went to live with a close friend of hers. She subsequently discovered that they had been having an affair for several months.

Circumstances of the overdose

After her husband's departure, Margaret had been feeling very miserable and frustrated, was having difficulty concentrating at work and had been avoiding her usual social contacts. She feared she would not be able to support her children. Her sleep had been very disturbed.

She had seen her general practitioner a week after the separation and he had prescribed a tranquillizer. However, her feelings of hopelessness increased over the next 3 weeks and late one night, after she had been drinking alone, she took an overdose of the tranquillizer mixed with paracetamol and then went to bed. She woke the following morning and took more tablets. Her son discovered her in a drowsy state an hour later.

Upon recovery in hospital she said she had intended to kill herself. Her Beck Suicidal Intent Scale score was 11 (moderately high).

The therapist interviewed her eldest son and telphoned her general practitioner. When interviewing Margaret, the therapist found her to be moderately depressed, but to an extent in keeping with her problems. He thought she had shown moderate suicidal intent in taking the overdose, particularly because she took it at night when unlikely to be discovered and repeated the act on waking in the morning. However, he also thought she might have been trying to demonstrate the extent of her distress to her family and possibly to her husband. Admission to a psychiatric unit was not thought necessary because she was able to make realistic plans concerning how she would cope during the next few days, and support was available from her children.

Initial problem list

1. Loss of husband.
2. After husband's departure: (i) failure to cope with children; (ii) failure to cope with full-time job; (iii) loss of social contacts.
3. Uncertainties about her financial circumstances and legal position.
4. Feelings of frustration, anger, and lack of energy.
5. Reluctance to ask for emotional support from either relatives or friends.
6. Insomnia.

The duration of all of these problems was 3 weeks.

Initial contract

Margaret agreed to be seen at home by the therapist initially for three sessions, to help her express her feelings of grief about the loss of her husband, and to explore ways of coping with her practical problems. The first session was arranged for 4 days later. Her general practitioner was agreeable to this plan.

Treatment

Session one

Margaret had returned to work by this time, but there had been no real change in her other problems. She talked about her husband and seemed to blame herself for his leaving. This discussion led to her becoming tearful and she was encouraged by the therapist to allow full expression of her distress. He explained that in allowing herself to cry she was showing a normal reaction to her loss and that this would lead to earlier resolution of her feelings than if she bottled them up.

She agreed to continue working and took the therapist's advice to contact a solicitor to deal with the legal aspects of the separation. She also said she would try to communicate more openly with her close relatives and friends. Because her sleep was still disturbed and her consequent lack of energy was making her job and domestic chores more difficult, the therapist said he would advise her general practitioner to prescribe a mild hypnotic, but that this would be for a strictly limited period.

Session two

Immediately after the previous session, Margaret had felt better, especially after starting to take the hypnotic. However, there had been some deterioration in her mood over the previous 2 days. This was due to two further difficulties. First, her solicitor had seemed unsympathetic and, secondly, her husband had written to let her know he wished to sell their house. On one occasion she had drunk a lot of alcohol, which had made her feel worse.

Margaret was encouraged to continue pursuing her enquiries with the solicitor. She agreed to avoid alcohol, and because the next session was not for a week, to telephone the therapist in 3 days time to inform him of her progress. This she did, at which stage she had managed to go without drinking, but had not yet been to see her solicitor.

Session three

Margaret had been coping a little better and her sleep pattern had returned to normal. She had been experiencing considerable feelings of grief about her husband and had been able to cry on occasions. In addition she had talked with relatives and friends about her difficulties.

The session was largely spent in helping her further to express her feelings of distress over the separation. Because her social isolation was made worse by her inability to drive she agreed, before the next session, to take the therapist's advice to arrange driving lessons.

Sessions four, five, and six

During these sessions she was further encouraged to express her feelings of grief. A dramatic change took place when she met and had a row with her husband. After this she ceased to blame herself for the breakdown of their marriage, but instead expressed considerable anger towards her husband. Her mood improved significantly as a result. On most nights she had been able to sleep without taking the hypnotic.

Margaret had started driving lessons, was making progress with the solicitor, and spending the occasional evening with friends. In addition, as the therapist had suggested, she had contacted the local Citizens' Advice Bureau to find out about evening classes.

Session seven

This took place 3 weeks later. In this final session Margaret was encouraged to explore possible ways of coping at times of further crises. She thought she would be able to telephone friends, whom she now realized were very keen to help her. Her mood was back to normal, although there remained some problems over her finances, and the legal situation was not entirely sorted out. Treatment was terminated and the general practitioner advised that the hypnotic could now be stopped.

Margaret continued to cope fairly well during the next year. Occasionally she became upset when reminded of her former marriage. She had been able to cope with the sale of her house. However, on the anniversary of her husband leaving home she drank heavily and took another overdose that night. The overdose did not appear to have involved serious suicidal intent. When seen in hospital she was far less depressed than on the first occasion and did not feel she needed further help. Therefore she was discharged.

Summary

The therapist was moderately successful in trying to help this woman experience a normal grief reaction after the loss of her husband. In addition, he was able to encourage her to tackle her other problems in a practical and sensible way. Nevertheless, despite considerable improvement in her social circumstances, she took a repeat overdose one year later. This illustrates a point discussed later (p. 181) that repeat overdoses often do occur despite apparent improvement in patients' social circumstances. In contrast with the previous case, where it was thought necessary to stop medication at the beginning of treatment, this woman clearly benefited from the introduction of a hypnotic for a brief period of time. Insomnia can severely undermine a person's ability to cope with other problems, including the stress of grieving.

CASE IV—AN ADOLESCENT WITH FAMILY PROBLEMS

Adolescents who take overdoses have considerable problems in their relationships with their parents. In the case described here, poor communication between an adolescent girl and both her mother and father resulted in mutual distrust. This case also illustrates the difficulties which can be encountered in carrying out treatment with adolescent self-poisoners.

Background

Pamela, aged 15, came from a family of four. Her father had a chronic heart condition as a result of which Pamela had come to feel that she could not discuss problems with him. She had become increasingly alienated from her mother and they were rowing a great deal. This was partly due to her parents' disapproval of her boyfriend. In addition, Pamela was concerned that her school work had deteriorated despite the considerable efforts she was making. She thought that her parents overestimated her ability to do well academically. She had a brother, aged 20, who had recently become engaged. Pamela had never felt close to him.

Circumstances of the overdose

On the day she took her overdose, Pamela had been taking her end-of-term examination in Biology and English, but thought that she had done very badly. She had arranged to see her boyfriend secretly that evening, but her mother suspected this and followed her. Pamela saw her mother trailing her and returned home without seeing her boyfriend. There she had a row with her mother after which she went to her bedroom, wrote a note saying how much she loved her boyfriend, and took an overdose of approximately 30 aspirin tablets and cut both her wrists superficially with a razor.

Her mother came up to her room a short while afterwards and found Pamela in a very distressed state with the empty bottle in front of her and blood on her clothing.

Assessment

When seen the next morning in hospital, Pamela said she had not cared whether she lived or died when she took the overdose, but had hoped that it would show her parents how upset she was feeling about her school work, and that it might also persuade them to change their attitudes to her boyfriend. Her score on the Beck Suicidal Intent Scale was 14 (fairly high).

She did not appear to be unduly depressed and now said that she thought the act had been rather drastic, but did not regret it. Although she was not suicidal the therapist agreed that she might have been feeling as if she wanted to die at the time of the overdose. The therapist also understood the behaviour in terms of Pamela's need both to show her parents how desperate she was feeling, and to try and change their behaviour towards her.

When Pamela's parents were interviewed they spent a lot of time emphasizing how necessary they thought it was to discipline Pamela. They said she overestimated how great their academic expectations for her were. The therapist suggested that many of the problems that had arisen were due to poor communication between Pamela and her parents, and that this had led to a sense of mistrust on both sides. She only saw Pamela and her parents together very briefly at this stage.

Initial problem list

1. Poor communication between Pamela and her parents (1 year).
2. Parents' intolerance of Pamela's relationship with boyfriend (1 month).
3. Pamela's lack of confidence in her academic ability and her feeling that she was letting her parents down (10 months).

Initial contract

The therapist agreed to see Pamela as an outpatient in 5 days' time to provide her with a further chance to talk about her difficulties and also to provide her with support. She thought that Pamela might benefit from having the opportunity to discuss her worries with someone outside the family. They agreed to meet for three or four sessions, after which a session would be held with her parents in order to assess progress and to help Pamela further improve her communication with them.

The plan was discussed with Pamela's general practitioner, who was in full agreement.

Treatment

Session one

During this session, 5 days after her discharge from hospital, Pamela talked further about her worries. She reported that since she had left hospital her parents had been more sympathetic towards her. However, she felt that this was artificial and did not reflect their real attitudes. She had been out with her boyfriend on one occasion and her parents had tried to be more accepting of her relationship with him. She had also passed the exam that she feared she would fail. The therapist suggested that possibly she tended to set herself standards that were too high and also underestimated her own ability. Pamela agreed that this was probably so. A further problem was identified at this time.

4. Pamela only had a few friends (1 year).

Pamela agreed that she would benefit from having new friends and said she would find out about youth clubs that existed in her area. She also said that she would ask her parents whether they would be happy about her going to a youth club with her best friend. This seemed a way in which she could begin to discuss things more openly with them.

Session two (8 days later)

Pamela had found out about two local youth clubs, one of which seemed particularly suitable for her. She agreed to attend this club the next week with her friend.

The therapist encouraged Pamela to make a list of ways in which she would like her parents to change in terms of providing her with greater freedom. She agreed to do this before the next session so that it could be discussed further and then used later in the conjoint session with her parents.

Session three (1 week later)

Pamela had joined the youth club and found it enjoyable. However, she had encountered difficulties in drawing up a list of ways in which she would like her parents to be more tolerant. During this session the therapist discussed with Pamela the reasonableness of her attitudes. For example, Pamela was surprised that her parents were concerned when a boy she had just met at a discotheque brought her home in the early hours of the morning. She seemed unwilling to acknowledge that this might not be wise and would be bound to cause her parents concern. The therapist tried to get her to look at such situations from her parents' viewpoint. She also asked Pamela to try again during the next week to draw up a list of ways she would like her parents to change.

Session four (1 week later)

Pamela said she had not done much thinking about her parents' attitudes. During this session the rapport between her and the therapist appeared to have deteriorated, and the therapist thought this was because Pamela was beginning to see her as aligned with her parents. The therapist suggested this to Pamela, who agreed that this might be so. However, she also agreed to attend a conjoint session with her parents the next week.

Session five

Both parents attended with Pamela. They seemed angry with the therapist although were not saying this openly. Pamela also appeared angry and seemed to wish the therapist to speak for her, which the therapist resisted. Instead she pointed out what she thought was happening in the session and the need for all of them to look at the problems in a constructive way. She said she thought the parents needed to be clear about what limits they felt they had to place on Pamela's behaviour. She pointed out that they rarely seemed to express affection towards Pamela and that this might be making her feel insecure. The therapist also suggested that Pamela should tell her parents more about what she was doing; for example, what time she planned to come home in the evening.

Some time was spent in discussion of the ways in which Pamela and her parents understood the reasons for the overdose. It was seen by the father solely as manipulative behaviour aimed at him and his wife. Pamela saw it more in terms of her need to show her parents how distressed she felt. The therapist encouraged them to consider the possibility that the act might be understood in terms of both these motives and that this highlighted the need for improved communication between them.

Finally, the parents were asked to make clear their attitudes towards Pamela's boyfriend. They reassured Pamela that they did trust her, but added that they hoped she would feel more able to be open with them about her social life. The parents did not want to attend any more sessions and treatment was therefore terminated.

Summary

This case provides an example of relatively poor use of brief treatment. It is clear that the therapist should have endeavoured at a much earlier stage to involve the parents in treatment, preferably by means of conjoint sessions with Pamela and her parents together. Although the therapist was probably correct in initially providing a chance for Pamela to express her worries to someone outside the family, she should have progressed as soon as possible to helping Pamela and her parents tackle together the problems surrounding their communication and lack of mutual trust. If the therapist had approached the problem in this way she may well have avoided alienating herself from both the patient and her parents and thereby becoming largely ineffective.

CASE V—A YOUNG MAN WITH PROBLEMS COMPLICATED BY UNEMPLOYMENT

As discussed earlier (p. 31), it is likely that unemployment can contribute to attempted suicide by precipitating or exacerbating domestic, social, and financial problems. The case described here illustrates brief counselling with a young man who had recently lost his job, and who was experiencing family and other problems.

Background

Tony was a 19-year-old single man living with his father and his father's girlfriend. Her 20-year-old son, Michael, who worked as an engineer, also lived in the house. Tony had been unemployed for 9 months, after the roofing firm he had been working with for a year had gone into liquidation. At first he had tried to look at the newspapers regularly to search for job vacancies and had sent application forms to prospective employers. However, for the last 6 months or so he had ceased to make regular efforts to find a job. The consequent reduction in his income had meant that he could not afford to run a car any longer, and therefore he had been seeing less and less of his girlfriend, who lived 15 miles away. One month before the overdose, she told him she wanted to end the relationship and he had reluctantly accepted this.

Circumstances of the overdose

Tony took the overdose on Sunday night, at around the time when his father, his father's girlfriend and her son were due to come back from the pub. Tony had decided not to go out with them, as he felt self-conscious about having to borrow money from his father to pay for drinks. He had drunk three glasses of home-made wine and had been trying to watch a film on television, but was unable to get interested in it. After attempting to speak to his ex-girlfriend on the telephone and finding she was out he decided to have another drink, and then started to think about taking some tablets which his GP had prescribed for him at the time when his girlfriend had left him. Tony's GP had prescribed the medication for his sleeping difficulties, but he had only taken it on two occasions, finding the tablets to be of little help. He had one further glass of wine and then took 16 nitrazepam tablets, leaving four in the bottle. He then returned to the sitting room and sat in front of the television where he was found asleep by his father and the others when they returned 40 minutes later. They found it difficult to rouse him and on seeing the bottle of tablets on the floor next to him, called an ambulance to take him to hospital.

Assessment

When Tony was seen in hospital by the therapist on the following morning he denied having wanted to kill himself, but claimed he was fed up and could not see any way out of his present difficulties. He was clearly embarrassed about what had occurred, but at first was unwilling to say much about what had happened. However, he opened up and discussed his problems with the therapist, at times bursting into tears. His score on the Beck Suicidal Intent Scale was 5 (low intent).

When Tony's father was interviewed he said he felt angry with Tony for having taken the tablets, especially as his girlfriend, Pat, had been with him when he found Tony unconscious. He also expressed irritation about the way Tony seemed to have let himself go in the last few months, since he had become unemployed. Pat was more sympathetic, but also admitted that she had become irritable with Tony now that he was spending so much time at home. After encouraging them to express their feelings, the therapist then explained how the change in Tony's behaviour and attitudes might be understandable in view of his current situation.

The therapist did not think that Tony was suffering from a psychiatric disorder, or that there was a risk of suicide, or of a further act of self-harm in the near future.

Initial problem list

Tony and the therapist agreed on the following problem list.

1. Problem coping with the break-up of his relationship with his girlfriend (1 month).

2. Unemployment, with consequent feelings of futility and hopelessness (9 months).

3. Deterioration of relationship with his father, his father's girlfriend, and son, Michael (4 months).

4. Social isolation (6 months).

Initial contract

Tony and the therapist arranged to meet four times during the next month. Tony did not want to involve his father or the rest of the family on a regular basis, but he was prepared to consider asking them to join the sessions at some stage, if necessary. The therapist informed the general practitioner of the plans.

Treatment

Session one

The first session took place 1 week later. Tony said he had felt happier after discharge from hospital and that his father had been less critical and more supportive during the last few days. His father had even telephoned his ex-wife to tell her about what had happened and she had then spoken to Tony, who had not heard from her for some months. Tony talked about his ex-girlfriend and then remembered how upset he had become when his parents split up when he was 14. At the time he had started to play truant at school and his academic progress had been disrupted. The therapist pointed out the parallels between the two situations: how he had reacted badly to the break-up of his parents' marriage, and now similarly to the end of his relationship with his girlfriend. Tony appeared to recognize a link between the two situations, which he had failed to appreciate until then. He added that he now felt more detached from his former girlfriend, and that he was already beginning to regard their relationship as belonging to the past.

Returning to the problem list, he felt the main problems he now had to deal with were his lack of job and his social isolation. After discussion with the therapist, Tony agreed to start searching for another job more systematically; he proposed to look at the local newspapers twice a week for possible job vacancies. He also agreed to start contacting some of his old friends whom he had lost touch with when he became unemployed.

Session two

Tony came back 10 days later looking happier, and reported that he had checked the newspapers regularly and had sent off several applications for jobs. He had been offered one interview, but had decided against it because, if he obtained the job, it would have meant travelling a long distance every day. However, he had continued to look regularly at the newspapers for other vacancies. He had also telephoned an old friend, who had invited him to a birthday party the following weekend, which he was looking forward to, although with some apprehension. He commented on how much nicer towards him the family seemed to be, including Michael, who had been telling him about his own problems at work. Tony also mentioned how he had visited a local centre for the young unemployed which he had seen advertised in the local newspaper. At first he had felt a little out of place, but had finally arranged to play football once a week with other members of the centre.

Session three

This took place 2 weeks later. At first Tony looked less happy than before, and said he had become somewhat despondent about his lack of progress in finding employment. However, he had persevered with the task and accepted it could be a while before he would find the kind of job he wanted. He reported having enjoyed the weekly game of football with other members of the youth unemployment centre. He had gone out to the pub a couple of times with some old friends and was thinking of taking out a young woman he had met. However, he was anxious about getting closely involved at present. Tony said he did not feel the need to come to see the therapist again, as he felt that he would now be able to tackle his difficulties without support.

The therapist encouraged Tony to look back at what had and had not changed, and stressed the efforts Tony had made to bring some structure and pleasure to his weekly routine, and to pursue his search for a job. Tony felt that one important factor had been the change in his father's attitude so that he now seemed to understand how he felt.

The therapist asked Tony to suggest how he would try to cope with similar problems in the future. Tony said he would not allow himself to get into the same state and that he would talk to someone about how he was feeling, probably his father or even his mother, and that he would try to do something active about his problems, rather than just giving up.

Summary

This case illustrates the sense of hopelessness that may develop in the unemployed, especially when finding a job appears to be an almost impossible task, and how this may create other problems, particularly when a major life event occurs, such as the break-up of an important relationship. The therapist's interventions, while relatively simple, contained several important elements of problem-solving. These included being prepared to listen and acknowledge

Tony's difficulties, helping his father and girlfriend view them in a more understanding way, after allowing them to ventilate their feelings, clarifying the nature of Tony's problems and helping him focus on those which he could do something about. The therapist's role was then largely one of encouraging him to persue tasks relevant to the problems and providing him with support while he was doing so. This case typifies how the brief problem-solving approach can be used in clinical work, not just with attempted suicide patients, but with many other people in crisis situations.

CONCLUSIONS

These five case examples have been described in detail to help the reader develop a clear understanding of the principles of assessment and brief problem-orientated treatment presented in the two previous chapters. Clinical experience has shown that the treatment approach can be used with approximately 30–40 per cent of patients referred to the general hospital after attempted suicide. It is also very well suited to the management of many patients with social and interpersonal problems who have not made attempts, but who are regularly encountered by psychiatrists, general practitioners, and social workers.

7

Psychiatric inpatient care of attempted suicide patients

INTRODUCTION

Although psychiatric inpatient care, either in a psychiatric hospital or in a psychiatric unit in the general hospital, is only necessary for a small proportion of attempted suicide patients (see Table 10), this group is particularly important because it includes the patients likely to be at greatest risk of subsequent suicide and some who pose particularly difficult management problems. Therefore, the whole of this chapter has been devoted to discussion of this aspect of care of attempted suicide patients.

Indications for psychiatric inpatient care

The types of patients likely to require psychiatric inpatient treatment were discussed in Chapter 4. To summarize, broadly speaking there are three main categories of such patients.

1. Those with serious psychiatric disorders, especially depression with serious suicidal ideation or significant impairment of insight. Also patients with schizophrenia, organic states, and some suffering from alcoholism.

2. Those at risk of suicide. The characteristics of such patients were described previously (p. 66). This group includes 'failed suicides'. It overlaps to a large extent with the first category.

3. Patients who require a short period of removal from stress. These include patients whose coping resources are temporarily exhausted, those who require further assessment, and patients for whom the mobilization of additional help is necessary before they can begin to cope with their difficulties.

The following case example is of a patient who was admitted to a psychiatric hospital because of reasons which placed her in both categories (1) and (2).

Margaret, a 58-year-old housewife, was admitted deeply unconscious to a general hospital after having taken a very large overdose of a mixture of tranquillizers, antidepressants, and paracetamol, together with half a bottle of vodka. She spent 5 days in the intensive care unit before recovery. On the day of the overdose, after her husband and daughter had gone to work, she had finished writing a suicide note which she had started a week before. After leaving the letter in a drawer she had gone to a nearby town and booked in at a hotel. Having asked that she should not be disturbed she had taken the overdose in her room. When her husband and daughter returned home they had been distressed at not finding Margaret. Eventually, they discovered the suicide note, which mentioned the name of the hotel. The police were contacted and they managed to find her.

During the assessment interview Margaret claimed she took the overdose intending to go to sleep and never wake up again. She was evasive when asked if she still felt like killing herself. However, she admitted that she had felt very miserable for 3 or 4 months. Recently, she had started thinking the future was hopeless and that she was no longer able to look after her husband and daughter properly. Her thoughts seemed slow and she complained of lack of energy and difficulty in staying asleep at night.

The therapist judged that Margaret had made a very serious attempt to kill herself, that she was severely depressed and a continuing suicide risk. Although Margaret felt that nothing could be done to help her she agreed to be admitted to a psychiatric unit.

For a few patients, compulsory admission to a psychiatric inpatient unit under an order of the Mental Health Act will be deemed necessary. Description of the types of patients for whom this might be indicated, and guidance on how to proceed were provided in Chapter 4 (p. 75). In addition, a summary of those sections of the Act concerned with admission of patients to hospital, or detention of patients already in hospital, which are relevant for attempted suicide patients was provided in an Appendix to that chapter.

THE NATURE OF PSYCHIATRIC INPATIENT TREATMENT

The phases of inpatient care and the forms of treatment available in the psychiatric hospital or psychiatric unit setting will now be considered. The discussion will be confined largely to general principles of treatment which should be applicable in most hospital settings, because a comprehensive description of all aspects of treatment is beyond the scope of this book. In addition, the specific details of treatment are bound to be influenced by the particular orientation or general approach of each individual unit or ward.

Initial period of admission

Every patient admitted as a psychiatric inpatient should be given a clear explanation beforehand of the purposes of the admission. The patient is then far more likely to respond favourably to the proposal than if the reasons for it are left vague. The therapist should enquire about any children, other dependent relatives, or pets that the patient may have and assist him to make appropriate arrangements for their care. The patient may also require advice on how to inform his employer about the admission. The patient's family doctor must be made aware that the admission is taking place. Preferably, the decision concerning admission should be taken in conjunction with him.

In their concern to help the patient, hospital staff sometimes show an unfortunate tendency to recommend the early introduction of antidepressant therapy. Usually, it is preferable if there are a few days of further careful assessment of the patient before such steps are taken. Apart from providing an opportunity for observing and talking to the patient, and thereby learning more about his problems and mental state, this initial period also has other purposes. First, further information about the patient can be obtained by interviewing relatives and acquaintances and from enquiry of any other hospitals where the patient has been treated. Secondly, the patient has time to develop confidence in staff members and other patients. Thirdly, changes in a patient's state are particularly likely to occur during this phase. Apart from being welcomed by the patient, such changes may also be very informative for staff. For example, quite often the mood of a patient who is severely depressed on admission will lift remarkably after admission. This does not mean that the admission was unjustified. However, it does suggest that the patient's distress beforehand was more likely to have been related to environmental stresses than an endogenous illness.

During this initial period it will be necessary to use whatever methods appear appropriate to deal with the patient's distress. The main approach will be through fairly frequent and prolonged human contact. This does not just mean interviews with a therapist, but also appropriate contact with nursing and other ward staff. The main role of the therapist at this stage will be to listen and to further his assessment by careful questioning. At the same time, realistic encouragement should be given to ensure that the patient remains hopeful about his eventual outcome. For the patient showing extreme distress, a tranquillizer may be indicated. Small doses of phenothiazines (e.g. chlorpromazine or thioridazine) are often the most appropriate. Because sleep is likely to be disturbed and insomnia can considerably worsen a patient's distress, it will often be helpful to prescribe an hypnotic. In either case the patient should be reassured that this is only a temporary measure.

Problem-orientated approach to care

The work of the clinical team is likely to be greatly assisted by use of a simple problem-orientated approach. Such an approach has several advantages. Through careful disentanglement of the patient's problems the action that is required to tackle his difficulties often becomes clearer. The process of clarification necessary to define the problem list can itself sometimes be helpful to the patient. Thus, seemingly infinite difficulties may be distilled into a few tangible problems. The problem list facilitates communication among staff members and helps clearly identify exactly who has agreed to do what and when. This is particularly useful when several staff members are involved in the patient's care. In addition, once the problem list is established together with the courses of action which have been agreed upon, review of the patient's progress, for example during ward rounds, is made relatively easy. Where the case is a complex one, subsidiary aspects of care are unlikely to be overlooked. Finally, the problem-orientated approach encourages clarity of thinking and planning which are essential ingredients in good patient care.

Sometimes it is incorrectly assumed that listing patients' problems precludes inclusion of psychiatric diagnosis. The use of a problem-orientated approach assists a therapist to get away from a purely medical or diagnostic approach because problems of a personal, social, medical, and psychiatric nature should all be included. If a patient has a psychiatric disorder this must be included in his list of problems, although sometimes the secondary effects of the illness are more important problems than the illness itself.

Table 12

Example of a problem list

Name of patient: John Smith   Age: 30   Date of admission: 15.3.85
Reasons for admission: serious salicylate and alcohol overdose; severely depressed; risk of suicide

Problem	Date of onset	Action
1. Depressive reaction (secondary to problems 2, 3, and 4): Feelings of inadequacy Loss of appetite Lack of energy	January 1985	(i) Supportive interviews by P.S. (doctor) to encourage patient to ventilate feelings, and to provide support and encouragement (ii) Daily mood chart (nurses)
2. Anger about wife's affair with her boss	January 1985	As for (i)
3. Uncertainty about future of marriage	January 1985	Exploratory interviews by M.T. (social worker) to assess wife's attitude
4. Threatened loss of job	December 1984	M.T. to contact employer—?patient likely to lose job
5. Insomnia (secondary to 1,2,3, and 4). Unable to get off to sleep	January 1985	Mild sleeping tablet if needed
6. Skin rash—red, blotchy, covering most of trunk	15 March 1985	P.S. to refer patient to to skin clinic

A simple form of problem list found useful in clinical practice is shown, together with a case illustration, in Table 12. Further examples were provided in summary form in Chapter 6. The problem list is most useful when it can be easily displayed at team meetings. There are several means of doing this. One is to have the list written out on a large piece of paper, which can be hung in a prominent position. Another is to record it on a transparency sheet, which can then be displayed by means of an overhead projector on a screen or blank wall. The latter has the advantages that the list can easily be amended and the transparency can be kept in the patient's notes.

Subsequent treatment

After the initial period of assessment and support it should be possible to formulate a treatment plan. The plan will vary according to the types of problem identified and the therapeutic approaches favoured by the staff in the ward. However, two broad, general approaches to treatment are available: *pschotherapeutic* and *physical*.

Psychotherapy

It is not pertinent here to discuss all possible psychotherapeutic approaches that might be used and their indications. Instead, the general principles of counselling the attempted suicide patient in the inpatient setting will be described.

The necessity for careful assessment and clarification of the patient's problems, and the therapeutic implications of such a procedure, have already been noted. Being prepared to *listen* while a patient expresses his concerns and distress is another important aspect of therapy. However, the therapist should also gradually try to *help the patient look constructively at ways of tackling the problems*. Thus, the aim with most patients should be to move eventually from assessment and support into a *problem-solving approach* as described in Chapter 5. Clearly, the patient is likely to be too distressed for such an approach early on in the admission.

During the course of counselling, patients who bottle up their feelings are often helped by being encouraged to express these emotions. The therapist can help such *ventilation* or *expression of emotions* by indicating that it is normal and appropriate both to have and to show such feelings. These are likely to include extreme sadness and anger. The therapist should be clear about his purpose in encouraging expression of bottled-up emotions. He may, for example, be aiming to help facilitate a patient's grief reaction after a loss, such as the break-up of his marriage. Another objective might be to help dissipate a patient's emotions sufficiently for him to be able to contemplate constructive approaches to tackling his problems.

It is also important that the patient be provided with realistic *encouragement*. The therapist should be alert to the possibilities of a patient losing all hope. This is a time when the risk of suicide or another attempt is likely to be high.

Therapeutic interviews at this stage need not be long; frequent, brief interviews (e.g. 20–30 minutes) are preferable to less frequent, but longer sessions. It can be useful to have one member of staff clearly designated as the patient's *primary therapist*. This person should whenever possible be the one who takes responsibility for counselling sessions. The patient should be aware of this, otherwise he is likely to turn to several members of staff to discuss his difficulties. This may result in his experiencing conflicting approaches and being given contradictory advice. This will in turn lead to confusion on the part of both staff and patient and is likely to hinder progress. In a setting where a multidisciplinary approach is practised, the primary therapist can be from any of the professions in the team. However, it is vital that the therapist, whatever his or her profession, has received satisfactory training in such counselling. Regular supervision should preferably be available. In addition the therapist will need to discuss the progress of the counselling with the rest of the team.

For patients with relationship difficulties, other approaches are likely to be indicated. Many patients will be having problems with their partners and for them conjoint treatment will often be appropriate. Others will have difficulties in relationships with other members of their families, in which case family therapy may be indicated. Although both conjoint and family therapy requires specific skills, such as avoiding taking sides, the general principles are similar to those already discussed. Conjoint therapy was considered in more detail in Chapter 5.

Physical treatments

Only the main principles involved in the use of physical methods of treatment during inpatient care of attempted suicide patients will be considered. The reader who wishes to have more detailed information on the various forms of physical treatments available should refer elsewhere. Crammer *et al.* (1982) have written a particularly useful guide to physical methods of treatment in psychiatry.

Because most attempted suicide patients have symptoms of depression, the most common decision concerning drug therapy will be whether to prescribe an *antidepressant*. The importance of not prescribing antidepressants immediately on admission has already been emphasized. It is all too easy to attribute changes in mood to drug therapy when in fact they have been the result of removing the patient from a stressful environment and providing him with support. The decision of whether to prescribe an antidepressant should be made on the basis of whether the patient shows 'biological' features of depression which predict a good response (e.g. early morning wakening, diurnal mood variation, and weight loss due to impaired appetite); whether, in the case of severe depression, one can afford to wait for the delayed response of an antidepressant; and the extent to which environmental factors seem largely to explain the symptoms.

If an antidepressant is indicated, it should be used in a full therapeutic dose and continued for an appropriate period of time. This is likely to be several months after full recovery. Availability of the medication should be under careful control in view of the dangers involved in overdosage. An antidepressant should never be the sole form of treatment a patient is receiving, even if his illness appears to be entirely of an endogenous variety. Such a patient will need support and encouragement, particularly during the two to three weeks before antidepressant effects are likely to occur. Most patients will also require counselling for social and personal difficulties.

Patients who experience recurrent depressive episodes of an endogenous nature, including those who also show hypomanic or manic mood swings, are likely to benefit from *lithium carbonate* therapy (Davis 1976). However, the primary use of lithium is for the prevention or reduction in intensity of *subsequent* episodes. It is of limited or no benefit for a current mood swing. Although Barraclough's (1972) suggestion that as many as a fifth of the suicides in a series he studied might have been prevented by the wider use of lithium would be difficult to substantiate and is probably an overestimate, the fact that the lives of as many as 16 per cent of patients with manic-depressive illness may end in suicide (Pitts and Winokur 1964) suggests that lithium is likely to have an important role in the prevention of suicide in some patients. Because of the potential side-effects and risks of lithium carbonate (e.g. toxicity, hypothyroidism, and renal impairment), as well the non-response of some patients, other drugs with possible prophylactic effects in patients with recurrent affective disorders are currently under investigation. These include carbamazepine (Post 1982) and sodium valproate (Puzynski and Klosiewicz 1984). At present there is no substantive evidence for their efficacy and lithium carbonate is still the first choice. Sometimes, a long-term antidepressant (e.g. amitriptyline or imipramine) may help prevent depressive episodes in people with recurrent unipolar affective disorders.

The use of *electroconvulsive therapy* (ECT) in carefully selected patients can rapidly relieve severe depression (Royal College of Psychiatrists 1977; Kendell 1981). ECT is likely to be indicated in severely depressed patients who show biological features of depression, especially if delusions or retardation are present (Brandon *et al.* 1984), and in whom it is felt that delay in relieving symptoms is unjustified. This would particularly apply where the risk of suicide is judged to be high. Recent evidence (Johnstone *et al.* 1980) suggests that the superiority of ECT over placebo treatment might be short-lived, but supports its use for immediate relief of symptoms. It is recommended that either antidepressant medication (Perry and Tsuang 1979) or lithium (Coppen *et al.* 1981) is introduced at the same time as commencing ECT to reduce the risk of relapse after the course of ECT is completed. The virtual outlawing of the use of ECT in some States in the USA has deprived suicidal depressed patients of an extremely effective and sometimes life-saving treatment. It is ironic that this prohibition occurred at the same time as several well-designed research studies were clearly demonstrating the efficacy of ECT.

Phenothiazine treatment will be required for the patient with an acute schizophrenic illness. The patient will also require supportive therapy, and his family is likely to need considerable help in understanding the illness and coming to terms with it. Relapse of schizophrenia seems to be more common in patients subject to extensive criticism or over-involvement by other family members (Vaughn and Leff 1976). Therapy aimed at amelioration of these behaviours can reduce the risk of relapse (Leff *et al.* 1982, 1985) especially if combined with family-orientated problem-solving (Falloon *et al.* 1982).

The patient who is suffering from alcoholism should preferably be admitted to a specialized treatment unit, if there is one available locally, so that expert help can be provided. An initial period of 'drying-out' may be necessary, with careful supervision and management of withdrawal symptoms. Treatment directed specially towards either stopping or reducing drinking on a long-term basis is very often thwarted by a patient's denial of the extent of the problem or by lack of motivation to do anything about it. Most patients who are suffering from alcoholism have considerable personal and social difficulties in addition. In some cases these may be amenable to the problem-solving approach described in Chapter 5, once drying-out has been completed.

Brief admission

Some patients benefit from brief admission to a psychiatric inpatient unit. The type of patient for whom this is indicated is one in an acute state of distress who is temporarily entirely unable to cope with his current problems. Typically, he will have just encountered a major and overwhelming life event, such as loss of a spouse through death or separation, be in a state of 'shock' and have resorted to self-poisoning or self-injury as an acute reaction to the event. Although probably not suffering from a serious psychiatric illness, he is likely to feel confused, angry, and (above all else) hopeless.

Such a 'crisis admission' might last from 2 days to a fortnight. Unfortunately, there is sometimes resistance among staff on inpatient units to admitting patients who may not be suffering from psychiatric illness, but who for a brief period of time need to hand over responsibility for their well-being to the inpatient clinical team. Often part of the resistance to the idea of brief admission is that the routine administrative procedures on a ward are geared to more long-term admission. It is most important that the purposes of such an admission are made clear to the ward staff beforehand.

The brief admission can serve several purposes. First, the patient's state of distress can be relieved by the support and care of staff and, where necessary, the use of tranquillizing or hypnotic medication. Secondly, it allows time for further interviews with relatives or friends in order to complete assessment of the patient's problems and likely supportive relationships. Thirdly, it provides an opportunity for careful planning of subsequent management, which is likely to consist of brief problem-orientated therapy as described in Chapter 5. The following case example illustrates a situation where such an admission seemed appropriate.

David, a 45-year-old married man employed on the production line of a car factory, was admitted to a general hospital after an overdose of 30 sleeping pills. A week before the overdose his wife Mary had left him and taken their two children with her. David tried to see her to persuade her to change her mind, but she refused any further contact with him. When he again tried to speak to her at her friend's home where she was staying, Mary called the police and they persuaded him to leave. The next day he went to work, but found he could not concentrate and returned home without telling anyone. After taking an overdose he told his neighbour what he had done and she called an ambulance.

During the assessment interview David was very distressed. He said he knew the tablets would not have harmed him and admitted that he had taken them to make his wife see how much he needed her. In the week since she had left he had slept poorly and spent much of the night pacing around the house. His general practitioner had prescribed the hypnotic 3 days before the overdose. He had not been eating properly and had been drinking more than usual.

The therapist did not think that the overdose had been associated with serious suicidal intent, nor that David was suffering from a psychiatric illness. However, there seemed to be a risk of a further overdose because it was clear that this one had not produced the desired effect. The therapist agreed to see David daily for the next few days in order to provide him with support. David said he would contact a solicitor to find out what his position was with regard to access to his children. He also agreed to talk to his father, who had helped him a good deal in the past. No hypnotic was prescribed in view of the risk of a further overdose. David was encouraged to return to work the next day because this seemed to be the one positive aspect of his current situation.

After being seen daily for 3 days David started to accept that his wife was not going to return home. This resulted in his becoming more distressed and unable to cope with either his work or looking after himself at home. His father confirmed his account. David was therefore offered inpatient care for up to 10 days to provide him with intensive support. It was agreed that he might return to work from the hospital when he felt better able to cope.

Occasionally, a patient requires repeated crisis admissions. The patient's history usually reveals long-standing difficulties in coping with stressful events and the use of maladaptive coping mechanisms, such as resorting to alcohol, regressing to a very dependent and helpless state, or inertia. Repeated self-poisoning or self-injury may also have occurred. It may have to be accepted that recurrent brief admissions are a necessary part of the long-term care of such a patient. Although these are likely to help prevent suicide, the risk of such a patient killing himself usually remains high. With this type of patient it is often necessary to take considered risks rather than treatment being entirely determined by suicide threats. The patient may develop a dependent relationship with one member of staff. This can be another necessary part of management. It is important that if this staff member should leave, his departure should be anticipated as early as possible and the patient helped to accept it, otherwise it is very likely to provoke another crisis and further admission.

Patients of this kind can be a considerable burden on staff. The rest of the team need to support the individual staff member who has the main therapeutic role. Sometimes a patient who is regarded as being totally dependent on hospital resources can cause a surprise by fairly suddenly changing, becoming relatively independent, and abandoning previous maladaptive coping behaviours. This is most likely to occur if the patient develops a supportive relationship with a partner, close friend, or voluntary worker.

Patients at special risk of suicide

The inpatient care of patients recognized as being at very high risk of suicide poses particular difficulties. This problem has become more obvious as hospitals have increasingly adopted the policy of having open wards. Observation and care of the patient at risk of suicide therefore needs to be very carefully planned and co-ordinated.

In most psychiatric units it is now usually considered inappropriate to have one member of staff constantly accompany a patient at risk. This reduces availability of staff for other purposes. In addition, the resulting sense of confinement and intense observation may increase a patient's feelings of hopelessness. It has even been suggested that such observation, especially if associated with low morale among staff, may actually increase the risk of suicide (Kobler and Stotland 1964).

On an open ward, the best arrangement for patients at risk is to have one area designated for their observation and management. This intensive care area should provide some degree of physical security by having the number of exits reduced to a minimum, preferably only one. It should also have a very high staff to patient ratio, with at least one staff member always present, even during changeover from one shift to another. This is a time when the risk of a suicide act may be greatest. Another time of risk is when there is a crisis on another part of the ward which distracts staff attention.

Some hospitals employ a set of policy rules for such patients whereby a particular level of precaution is nominated for each patient according to the extent of risk (Morgan 1979). The levels of precaution differ in the amount of freedom the patient is allowed and the intensity of observation. The level of precaution is regularly reviewed in the light of the patient's progress. Whatever approach is taken to the patient at special risk of suicide it is most important that all members of staff involved in the patient's care are absolutely clear about the current policy at all times. If they are not the risk of a tragic outcome is more likely.

Understandably, some nursing staff, especially those who are more junior, feel very uncomfortable in the role of providing the vigilant observation needed for patients at risk of suicide. It may be helpful, therefore, to ensure that all staff on the ward take a turn working in the intensive care area. However, the advantages of such an arrangement must be weighed against the potential disadvantages of there not being particular nurses who get to know the at-risk patients really well. If some staff do feel uncomfortable in this role they should have the opportunity to discuss their feelings with other members of the team. They may be helped by being reminded of the long-term benefits of such observation.

Attempted suicide and suicide in hospital

It is well recognized that, despite careful precautions, self-poisoning and self-injury do occur among psychiatric inpatients (Hawton 1978). This is sometimes a source of surprise and anger to those unfamiliar with inpatient care, yet when one examines the reasons more closely there is little cause for surprise. First, many patients in hospital have taken overdoses or injured themselves in the past. As many as a third of a consecutive sample of psychiatric hospital inpatients in one study were found to have such a history (Hawton 1978). Secondly, admission to a psychiatric unit has presumably been the result of distress which in many cases will persist after admission. This is the time when self-poisoning or self-injury are most likely. Finally, there is the strong possibility that a contagion effect will operate in this setting. Patients at risk may be more likely to take an overdose or injure themselves if aware both of such behaviour by others and the increased attention from staff and patients which usually results. This may partly explain why self-poisoning and self-injury among patients sometimes occur in 'epidemics' (Hawton 1978). If an outbreak of self-poisoning and self-injury starts on a ward, the staff need first to try to understand why it is happening. Sometimes one, possibly two patients, appear to be central to the outbreak and should, if possible, be moved to another setting. Open discussion of the phenomenon with all patients on the ward is recommended.

Unfortunately this behaviour is not confined to non-fatal attempts; suicides also occur in hospital (Levy and Southcombe 1953; Hawton 1978; Crammer 1984). Indeed, the risk on acute psychiatric units has been estimated at over 50 times the risk in the general population (Fernando and Storm 1984). Contrary to suicide patterns in the general population, younger patients may be most at risk, but in keeping with suicide in the general population, men are more at risk than women. The greatest risk in men is found in those with affective illnesses or schizophrenia; in women the highest risk is in those with affective illnesses and/or personality disorders (Copas and Robin 1982). A history of attempted suicide is a particular risk factor (Roy 1982; Fernando and Storm 1984), although, as noted above, this applies to at least a third of hospital patients. It has been suggested that alienation from others (both staff and patients) on the ward often precedes suicide (Morgan and Priest 1984). The hospital environment might also be conducive to certain forms of suicide [e.g. a high building (Salmons 1984), adjacent railway track (Langley and Bayatti 1984) or river]. The week following admission appears to be the time of greatest risk (Copas and Robin 1982).

Suicides in hospital patients are tragic events, causing distress to staff and other patients. Some patients may feel extremely insecure and show anger towards the staff. The staff in turn are likely to experience guilt and a profound sense of failure. Sometimes the act has been carried out in a hostile fashion that causes maximum distress to the staff. The main danger in the staff reaction is that there might be a severe loss of morale which can affect the care of other patients.

The following approach to the management of the consequences of a death by suicide of a patient while in hospital is recommended. First, the event should be openly discussed with patients on the ward so that they can air their anxieties and be given support. Secondly, the staff on the ward will themselves need assistance in coping with their own feelings about the tragedy. The team leader is usually the most appropriate person to provide this, and can probably best do so in the setting of group discussion with staff members. Finally, a 'psychiatric post-mortem' might be held some weeks later when staff feel less distressed. This would consist of a meeting of staff, preferably with a chairman not directly involved with the work of the team, in which staff members would be encouraged to contribute information concerning the patient and his circumstances which would enable a full picture of the events leading up to the suicide to be established. The aim of such a meeting would not be to see whether any staff members have particular responsibility for the event but to try to develop a shared understanding of why it occurred. This information may be helpful when the team is faced with the care of similar patients in future.

Care on discharge

A carefully planned programme of subsequent care should be
arranged before a patient is discharged from psychiatric inpatient
treatment. Clearly, the range of possible plans is very diverse. One
patient might attend the ward as a day-patient, another may be seen
with his partner for marital therapy, another may continue in
individual problem-orientated therapy, and so on. It is important to
remember that whatever type of subsequent care is to occur, the
period after discharge may be a time of particular difficulty. Many
of the stresses that led to admission may be encountered again. This
may be made worse if the patient feels stigmatized because he has
been a psychiatric inpatient. For depressed patients there appears to
be an increased risk of suicide immediately after discharge from
hospital (Pokorny 1964).

CONCLUSIONS

Although the proportion of deliberate self-poisoning or self-injury
patients who require psychiatric inpatient care is fairly small, this
group is of special importance because it includes those most likely
to have serious psychiatric disorders, those at special risk of suicide
or further attempts, and some patients who pose very difficult
management problems. A case has been made for brief admission of
patients who may not be suffering from psychiatric disorders, but
who are in a state of particularly severe crisis. Clearly, the decision
to admit a patient to hospital must be taken only after very careful
consideration.

When a patient is admitted to a psychiatric inpatient unit the
clinical team should avoid the temptation to commence specific
treatments immediately, especially those of a physical nature. Better
management is likely to result from a period of careful observation
and assessment, with considerable support being provided at this
time through frequent contact with nursing and other ward staff. A
simple problem-orientated metod of assessment can facilitate both
management and communication between staff members. In units
which employ a multidisciplinary approach, each patient might be
allocated one member of staff (a 'primary therapist') who has the
main responsibility for dealing with the patient's problems. This
should avoid conflicting advice or approaches. Above all else, it is

important that psychiatric inpatient care is based on a carefully co-ordinated policy, especially for patients at particular risk of suicide. If a suicide should occur in hospital it is recommended that attention is paid to dealing with the resultant feelings both of patients and staff.

8

Self-injury

The vast majority of patients referred to general hospitals because of acts of self-harm have taken overdoses. There is also a very important smaller group who have deliberately injured themselves in some way. The size of this group varies in different centres according to the method of detection of self-injury patients. In Edinburgh (Kreitman 1977) and Bristol (Morgan *et al.* 1975a), patients with self-injuries have constituted approximately 5 per cent of the total number of attempted suicide patients identified on the basis of general hospital referrals. However, the number of self-injuries identified in Edinburgh through referrals to the Regional Poisoning Treatment Centre may have been an underestimate of the total number of cases referred to hospital (Kreitman 1977), and, in addition, a high proportion of patients with self-injuries may not be referred to hospital at all (Kennedy and Kreitman 1973).

In Oxford, particular care has been taken to try to identify all cases of self-injury coming to the general hospital, irrespective of whether they have been referred to the hospital psychiatric service. Of over 4000 consecutive general hospital referrals for self-poisoning and self-injury during the 5 years from 1980 to 1984, 13 per cent involved self-inflicted injuries. The types of injuries and the methods used vary widely, as is illustrated in Table 13. Similarly, the patients who injure themselves do not form a homogeneous group, but include individuals who can to a large extent be classified into three subgroups on the basis of the type of injury inflicted and the associated degree of suicidal intent:

1. *Superficial self-cutting*, usually of the wrist or forearm, associated with little or no suicidal intent.
2. *Serious self-injury*, such as deep cutting—which may endanger major blood vessels, nerves, and tendons—and shooting, hanging, and jumping from buildings, all of which are usually associated with serious suicidal intent.

Table 13

Details of self-injuries in patients referred to the general hospital in Oxford, 1980–84. Results are given as numbers of patients, with percentages in parenthesis

Type or method of injury	Males	Females	Total
Cut wrist/forearm	211 (75)	233 (86)	444 (80)
Cut elsewhere	25 (9)	11 (4)	36 (7)
Gunshot/drowning/ asphyxiation (including hanging)	19 (7)	16 (6)	35 (6)
Jumping from a height	11 (4)	8 (3)	19 (4)
Jumping in front of a moving vehicle	7 (2)	0 (0)	7 (1)
Other	9 (3)	4 (1)	13 (2)
Total	282 (100)	272 (100)	554 (100)

3. *Self-mutilation*, which may result in disfigurement. This usually occurs in individuals with psychotic illnesses, such as schizophrenia, and may or may not endanger life.

These three groups will now be considered in more detail, although most attention will be paid to the first group because this includes by far the majority of self-injury patients.

SUPERFICIAL SELF-CUTTING

Incidence

It is unclear how common self-cutting is. Although at least 80 per cent of patients referred to the general hospital in Oxford after self-injury have cut themselves superficially, it seems likely that many more episodes of deliberate self-cutting occur than are identified through general hospital records. For example, superficial cutting occurs quite often in psychiatric inpatient settings, sometimes in epidemics (Simpson 1975), and the vast majority of such episodes do not necessitate general hospital treatment (Hawton 1978). Some cases of self-cutting which reach casualty departments are mis-identified as accidental lacerations. Therefore, the full extent of this behaviour is uncertain. Nevertheless, there have been several studies of patients who cut themselves which are very informative for the clinician (Clendenin and Murphy 1971; Rosenthal *et al.* 1972; Simpson 1975).

Characteristics of people involved in self-cutting

The typical self-cutter has been described as a young, single, attractive female who repeatedly cuts her wrist or forearm. However, the extent to which this is a typical case has been questioned (Clendenin and Murphy 1971; Weissman 1975). Reference to Table 13 indicates that almost as many males as females are referred to hospital after self-cutting. The Table also shows that cutting usually involves the wrist or forearm, which has resulted in wrist-cutting being treated as a distinct syndrome (Rosenthal *et al.* 1972). It is doubtful whether this is a useful approach to the problem, especially for clinical purposes.

Although most patients who cut their wrists have experienced psychiatric symptoms, they do not fit into any one category of psychiatric diagnosis. Many have considerable personality difficulties, and the most commonly applied diagnosis is 'personality disorder'. Unfortunately this diagnosis is often used non-specifically; it also tends to promote a sense of therapeutic nihilism. In the USA the DSM III diagnosis of 'borderline personality disorder' (p. 35) would often be used for such individuals. Many self-cutters have depressive symptoms, but the highly transient nature of these does not suggest serious depressive illness. The picture is often one of violent and rapid mood swings in response to stress. The stress is usually an actual or perceived rejection, which activates the individual's underlying sense of worthlessness.

A very interesting association appears to exist between cutting and eating disorders, which were found in 15 (65 per cent) out of 23 cutters studied by Rosenthal *et al.* (1972), and in 18 (75 per cent) out of 24 patients reported by Simpson (1975). The eating disorders include compulsive overeating and severe anorexia, both being found in some patients. Cutting may occur at the time of binge-eating. Many self-cutters also abuse alcohol or drugs (Simpson 1975).

Another interesting finding is that many of these patients have worked in the medical field; they are particularly likely to be or have been nurses (Simpson 1975). At present there is no explanation for this.

Background

Cutters often come from broken homes, although perhaps no more often than attempted suicide patients in general (Rosenthal *et al.* 1972). Deprivation of parental warmth and physical contact have been emphasized by other workers (Simpson 1976). Some patients have a history of hospitalization and surgery before the age of 5, and in some cases such events have occurred before the age of 18 months (Rosenthal *et al.* 1972; Simpson 1975). A greater number than would be expected have spent long periods in plaster casts because of bone injuries, or for correction of congenital mal-formations.

Disturbances of menstruation are also commonly reported (Rosenthal *et al.* 1972; Simpson 1975). These include negative reactions to the onset of menstruation, dislike of menstruation, and menstrual irregularity (this last feature may be the result of an eating disorder). There is dispute as to whether cutting is more likely at the time of menstruation (Simpson 1976).

There is less doubt about the occurrence of sexual problems. Confusion of sexual identity and lack of enjoyment of sexual relationships are often found (Rosenthal *et al.* 1972; Simpson 1975; Gardner and Gardner 1975).

Some workers have emphasized the difficulty most of these patients experience in expressing their emotional needs (Simpson 1976). Others, using questionnaires to evaluate personality traits, have suggested that many cutters have obsessional personalities (McKerracher *et al.* 1968; Gardner and Gardner 1975).

In animals, disturbances of neurotransmitters can cause behavioural changes which may include self-mutilation. Because of this, and because there are rare human disorders in which self-mutilation may be a feature (e.g. Lesch-Nyhan, deLange, and Tourette's syndromes), and which may result from neurotransmitter changes, it is possible that neurotransmitter disturbances may contribute to self-cutting. Furthermore, absence of pain during cutting (see below) raises the possibility that endorphins have a role in the phenomenon. However, at present these suggestions remain purely speculative.

The act of cutting

Cutting is typically of the wrist or forearm, and the cuts are usually multiple. They vary from superficial scratches to full-thickness lacerations, but almost invariably draw blood. The cuts are usually made with razor blades or broken glass. Other forms of self-mutilation may be seen in the same patient. These include cuts elsewhere on the body, such as the legs and genital areas, and cigarette burns and bruises. Most cutters engage in the behaviour on several occasions, some cutting themselves hundreds of times altogether (Rosenthal *et al.* 1972).

Common precipitants for the behaviour are actual or threatened loss or abandonment, or an impasse in a personal relationship (Simpson 1975). The act is usually preceded by feelings of anger, self-hatred, and sometimes depression. The predominant sensation is one of tension, which steadily mounts until it becomes unbearable. The patient will usually seek out solitude at this time. Immediately before cutting, a sense of numbness or emptiness may be described. In some cases, depersonalization (a sense of detachment between mind and body) or dissociation (a disturbance of conscious awareness) seem to occur. The cut may be made with little or no apparent awareness, the patient suddenly discovering that she has cut herself and at the same time experiencing a sense of relief. The sight of blood seems to be an important component of the process, and it often provides the patient with the sense of relief which may be mingled with feelings of disgust or guilt. Most patients rarely report experiencing pain during the act of cutting.

The cut often rapidly reduces tension and brings a sense of returning to reality. The tension-relieving effect of cutting may be extremely important when one is considering therapeutic strategies to counter the behaviour. Only very rarely has the patient carried out the act with suicidal intent in mind.

Self-cutting is sometimes a problem in inpatient psychiatric units, especially those catering for adolescents, where it may occur in an epidemic fashion (Simpson 1975; Walsh and Rosen 1985). Learning through modelling and competition between patients are likely to be important factors in such epidemics.

Case example

Jenny, a single girl aged 27, had experienced an unhappy childhood. Her parents got on badly, and she described her mother as extremely cold and rejecting. She had always been an anxious individual and during her teens she went through periods of compulsive overeating alternating with dieting. She also showed obsessional traits, including rituals concerned with dressing, washing, and general checking. Her general practitioner had at one time treated her unsuccessfully for this with an antidepressant.

Jenny had formed relationships with several boyfriends, but these usually ended because she became over-dependent. She had never derived any pleasure from sex, which she regarded with a mixture of lack of interest and revulsion.

At the age of 20 she took an overdose when she thought a boyfriend was about to desert her. She was offered psychotherapy, but this proved ineffective and it was concluded that Jenny lacked insight into her problems. From the age of 22 she had cut herself on many occasions. The cuts were always superficial and usually consisted of between 20 and 40 neat parallel scratches on her wrist and forearm. The behaviour was similar on each occasion. Jenny once explained, 'It's a ritual and must be done correctly'. She experienced a sense of detachment before cutting herself, and the act seemed to relieve feelings of anxiety and tension which usually arose from problems in her relationship with her boyfriend. At the same time, cutting acted as a kind of punishment which, because of her sense of worthlessness, Jenny felt she needed.

Management

There is general agreement that the management of patients who cut themselves, especially those who often repeat the behaviour, can be difficult and that there is a need for the development and evaluation of new forms of treatment. At present, only general guidelines to management can be provided, based largely on the characteristics of the behaviour which have been described.

Two lines of approach appear to be most hopeful. The first involves teaching the patient alternative means of dealing with the feelings of tension which precede cutting, and the second involves psychotherapeutic measures aimed at improving the patient's self-esteem, and her ability to communicate feelings and needs. These are not necessarily alternative methods of management; success is probably most likely where both are utilized. The use of tranquillizers of either the major (e.g. phenothiazines) or minor groups (e.g. benzodiazepines) does not usually appear to be helpful.

Methods of reducing tension

The aim here would be to enable the patient to recognize the common precipitants of the feelings which precede cutting and then to take appropriate action to prevent these feelings mounting up to the state of extreme tension which is associated with cutting. Before suggesting methods of countering the development of tension, careful assessment of the antecedents to cutting should be carried out. These include the events which precede it and the way in which the patient's feelings develop. Detailed analysis of this kind should enable the most appropriate method of tension reduction to be chosen for each individual patient.

For this approach to succeed, the patient must want to gain control over her feelings, and be motivated sufficiently to practise the techniques that are suggested. This is very important because the act of cutting usually has immediate effects on tension and is also likely to evoke responses from other people which may serve to strengthen the urge to cut.

One approach to tension reduction is to teach the patient methods of self-relaxation. The use of progressive muscle relaxation exercises, as in the Jacobsen technique (1938) commonly employed in systematic desensitization, is a possible method. For these to be effective the patient would need to practise them repeatedly to be able to bring about fairly rapid relaxation when tense feelings were beginning to occur. An audio-tape recording in which the exercises are described can be a useful adjunct to teaching the patient this method, provided the therapist has first demonstrated the procedure to the patient, and the technique has been learned adequately.

Relaxation alone is unlikely to prevent cutting in most cases. The patient may also benefit from learning methods of distraction which can be used to interrupt the flow of negative thoughts which often accompany the build-up of feelings of tension. These would include practising counter-thoughts in which alternative ways of viewing the situation are entertained, and switching to prerehearsed thoughts of circumstances in which the patient has felt particularly relaxed.

Another approach would be to help the patient find other means of discharging tension. Vigorous exercise is one. Venting feelings through non-harmful means, such as punching a rubber object, is another. The use of rubber bands on the wrist which can be flicked to produce pain, but no damage is a further possibility. Rosen and Thomas (1984) have suggested that repeatedly squeezing a small rubber ball in the hand until this produces considerable discomfort in the wrist and forearm can also help.

These are techniques which require development and evaluation. It is unlikely that any one method would suit all patients and therefore it is best to discuss with the patient alternative approaches to find out which seems the most likely to succeed.

One further method of tension reduction which is of interest has been described by Graff and Mallin (1967). They found that in some patients, self-cutting could be prevented by the provision of physical contact by a therapist, such as in putting an arm round the patient. This might be useful for the psychiatric inpatient who cuts repeatedly, although the limits of therapist-patient contact would have to be very clear.

Psychotherapy

In the management of the self-cutter who often repeats the behaviour it is sensible for one therapist to establish a relationship with the individual. This will prevent conflicting messages and advice being given. However, the therapist will benefit from being able to discuss the case with other members of the team or a supervisor in order to be given support and guidance.

The psychotherapeutic management of the self-cutter is difficult and challenging, but in many cases well worth trying. This should include an attitude of acceptance on the part of the therapist towards the patient's problems and behaviour, while at the same time limits will need to be set in terms of what the therapist is able to provide and tolerate. The goals would include development of the patient's self-esteem through encouraging the positive aspects of personality, and helping the patient to communicate needs and feelings verbally. Clearly, good rapport between patient and therapist will be necessary, but the patient will also have to develop confidence in the therapist. The pursuit of analytical insights into the reasons for cutting is probably unhelpful (Simpson 1976). However, a cognitive therapy approach to helping the patient understand and reappraise her feelings of worthlessness may be worth trying (Beck *et al.* 1979). This involves helping the patient develop alternative and less self-blaming ideas about how other people behave towards her, and examining with her the origins and validity of her underlying sense of worthlessness.

In addition to the measures described, the therapist should also endeavour to help the patient start to adopt a problem-solving approach to current difficulties along the lines described in Chapter 5.

Outcome

There is hardly any information available concerning the long-term outcome of patients who cut themselves. In one study of a small group of wrist-slashers it was found that more than half were well, or had shown improvement, 5–6 years later (Nelson and Grunebaum 1971). However, there were other patients whose lives had ended in suicide. These were very disturbed patients who perhaps do not fit into the group under discussion here. Nevertheless, clinical experience suggests that the risk of eventual suicide even in 'typical' self-cutters is often high.

SERIOUS SELF-INJURY

Probably most serious attempts at suicide in which some form of self-injury is inflicted result in death. Nevertheless, as can be seen in Table 13, a small proportion of patients admitted to the general hospital after self-injury have used very dangerous methods (e.g. jumping from buildings, jumping in front of vehicles, hanging, and drowning) and yet have survived. In addition, there are a few patients who have survived after inflicting deep cuts, usually of the throat and neck. Patients in this group are likely to be older males. Serious suicidal intent is usually involved in their acts (although, as discussed earlier (p. 17), even shooting may occur when there appears to be ambivalence about dying). Many are suffering from severe depressive illnesses, often with persecutory ideas or delusions. Some are alcoholics.

Case example

A 57-year-old man, who had been forced to retire from work

because of chronic ill health, was admitted to hospital having made severe lacerations of his neck with a knife. He had been discovered unconscious in his kitchen by his son-in-law. The deep cuts had missed the major blood vessels and nerves in his neck, but had caused considerable blood loss. Upon recovering, he admitted he had been extremely depressed since the death of his wife from cancer a year earlier and now did not think he had anything to live for. He agreed to be admitted to a psychiatric unit where, after 2 months' treatment with psychotherapy and antidepressants, he appeared to improve considerably. However, after discharge from hospital he remained isolated despite efforts that were made to encourage him to develop social contacts through joining community clubs. Five months later he was found dead in his garage, having hanged himself.

Because most patients who inflict serious self-injuries are suffering from psychiatric disorders and are usually at high risk of making another attempt, the principles of management are largely those described in Chapter 7 where psychiatric inpatient care was considered. The clinician should be alert to the possible repetition of a serious attempt in hospital. In addition, it should be remembered that the occurrence of suicide in such patients while in the general medical ward is not unknown.

Occasionally, serious self-injury has particularly dire consequences when the injury itself causes permanent physical deformity. This is not unusual where a method such as jumping from a building has been employed. In addition, deep lacerations may result in disfiguring scars. The deformity or disfigurement may be an added cause for depression and regret at having failed in the attempt.

SELF-MUTILATION

Although not entirely distinct from the previous two categories, there is a small group of patients who turn up in casualty departments having inflicted mutilating injuries on themselves as a result of a serious disturbance of mental state. Included in this group are schizophrenic subjects who have injured themselves as a consequence of a delusional belief (for example, that part of the body was evil), or because of an hallucination (such as one in which voices tell the subject to harm himself). The target for the injury is not infrequently the genital area (Kushner 1967), although other parts of the body, including the eyes, can be involved.

Self-mutilation of the genitals very occasionally occurs in trans-sexual patients in an attempt to initiate sex change. One such patient, a man of low intelligence, aged 39, was admitted to hospital after almost competely removing one of his testicles with a razor blade. At first he gave the somewhat fatuous explanation that he thought he would find it easier to ride his bicycle without his testicle (the other testicle was small due to atrophy). On closer questioning it was found that he had been harbouring strong trans-sexual feelings for some while and that the injury resulted from an urge to initiate a sex change.

The management of patients who mutilate themselves while in a disturbed state will include treatment of the disorder that has led to the disturbance and will invariably have to be initiated in the psychiatric inpatient setting.

CONCLUSIONS

Deliberate self-injury is far less common that deliberate self-poisoning among referrals to the general hospital. Nevertheless, within the group of patients who injure themselves three subgroups can be discerned. The first, and by far the largest group, is made up of those who cut their wrists and arms. In many cases this seems to be a means of tension reduction, and management must be directed partly towards developing alternative means of dealing with feelings of tension and partly to helping alleviate the ideas of worthlessness, as well as other problems, often experienced by such patients. The second group comprises patients who inflict serious injuries on themselves with considerable suicidal intent. The third group includes patients who mutilate themselves, usually in the context of a serious psychiatric illness. Members of clinical teams which manage attempted suicide patients should be familiar with the special problem of patients who deliberately injure themselves, and not just deal with them as if the behaviour was the same as self-poisoning.

9

Practical organization of services

The problem of deliberate self-poisoning and self-injury has placed enormous pressure on the staff (physicians, nurses, psychiatrists) and services (casualty and emergency departments, medical admission units, psychiatric and social work departments) involved in the care of patients who take overdoses or injure themselves, and this has been one of the factors that has promoted a re-examination of previously accepted policies for the management of attempted suicide patients. However, the new approaches are not simply a response to administrative or organizational problems. They reflect changes in the population of attempters, with a possible decline in the proportion of patients suffering from formal psychiatric illness while, instead, interpersonal conflicts and social problems play a prominent part in most cases. They are also indicative of more general changes in the role of psychiatrists and other professionals, such as social workers and psychiatric nurses, in the direction of better collaboration and sharing of skills between the different professional groups. As a result, the alternative models proposed to deal with the needs of the large number of patients brought to general hospitals after suicide attempts have included a reassessment of the role of psychiatrists, physicians, and non-medically qualified therapists.

In the United Kingdom, the current policy for attempted suicide patients is contained in guidelines issued by the Department of Health and Social Security (DHSS 1984). Before describing the current guidelines in detail, it is worth reviewing the policy changes that have taken place over the last two decades. Attempted suicide ceased to be a criminal offence with the implementation of the Suicide Act in 1961. In the words of the circular issued by the Ministry of Health (1961): 'Attempted suicide is in the future to be regarded entirely as a medical and social problem. . . . Hospital authorities are therefore asked to do their best to see that all cases of attempted suicide brought to hospital receive psychiatric investigation before discharge.' A comprehensive review of the problem of attempted suicide and its management was carried out a few years later by a committee chaired by Sir Denis Hill. Amongst other recommendations, the Hill Report (Central and Scottish Health Services Councils 1968) advocated the establishment of poisoning treatment centres in district general hospitals to which all cases of deliberate self-poisoning should be referred, no matter how serious the medical condition of the patients. Also, it recommended that psychiatric emergency cover should be available every day of the week, and that a psychiatric history and examination be completed for each patient as soon as possible. Social work help should be provided on a similar basis, and there ought to be continuity of care after discharge. The report recognized that in hospitals without a psychiatric unit the initial psychiatric and social evaluation might have to be undertaken by staff from the local psychiatric hospital.

One such poisoning treatment centre was developed in Edinburgh, and Matthew *et al.* (1969) have described its structure and functions. Reservations were soon expressed, however, about the necessity for psychiatrists to carry out the assessments in view of the relatively small number of patients who suffered from psychiatric illness and the pressures on already stretched psychiatric resources (Crammer 1969). The need for regional and district poisoning treatment centres was also questioned, and Lawson and Mitchell (1972) showed how an acute medical unit without special facilities could meet the recommendations contained in the Hill Report.

The value of one of the principal recommendations, the provision of psychiatric care to attempted suicide patients, remains controversial, and it has only recently been subjected to controlled evaluation (Hawton *et al.* 1987). Early evidence supporting psychiatric intervention came from non-randomized, retrospective studies (Greer and Bagley 1971; Kennedy 1972), and more work is required to establish which patients are likely to benefit from psychiatric care. The question of the efficacy of psychiatric intervention is discussed more fully in Chapter 10.

The official recommendation on psychiatric referral tended to be disregarded in practice. Thus, patients were not always being admitted to hospital and, when admitted, had not always been referred to a psychiatrist. In hospitals without a psychiatric unit, patients usually had to wait several days before being seen by the psychiatrist, occupying medical beds and often antagonizing the medical staff by their presence. In the meantime, the number of suicide attempters referred to hospitals has continued to present an organizational challenge. It is against this background that the new approaches to the psychiatric management of attempted suicide and the new official policy have to be considered.

In 1984, a multidisciplinary working party which included representatives from psychiatry, general medicine and surgery, paediatrics, nursing, social work, and psychology, carried out a review of developments in the management of 'deliberate self-harm' (attempted suicide), and made recommendations which were backed by the Department of Health (DHSS 1984). One of the main recommendations was the acknowledgement that non-psychiatrists (general physicians, social workers, and psychiatric nurses) could undertake the psychosocial management of attempted suicide patients. The report also emphasized the need for adequate training and supervision of personnel working in this area. Detailed advice about the organization of local services is contained in the report, together with the recognition of the needs of children and adolescents who harm themselves. The recommendations concerning the management of young suicide attempters echoed the views of the Royal College of Psychiatrists (Royal College of Psychiatrists 1982).

The clinical and research developments which have led to changes in the official policy will now be described.

ASSESSMENT

Who should assess suicide attempters?

Assessment has traditionally been regarded as the responsibility of psychiatrists, but in recent years the role of non-medically qualified personnel has been examined. Newson-Smith and Hirsch (1979b) compared assessments by social workers and psychiatrists in terms of recognition of psychiatric disorder, evaluation of motives, physical illness, and recommendations for immediate management. They found there was good agreement between both groups, although social workers tended to be more cautious in their judgements. Thus, for example, they were more likely than the psychiatrists to diagnose psychiatric disorder or recommend inpatient care. Newson-Smith and Hirsch concluded that social workers could safely and reliably assess attempted suicide patients. In addition, the social workers in their study appeared to be more aware than the psychiatrists of the relevance of interpersonal and family problems, a clear advantage considering the importance of such social difficulties for these patients. It was therefore suggested that social workers should be involved in assessment of attempted suicide patients, the psychiatrist being available to deal with emergencies and for consultation with the social worker if necessary.

An alternative system involving nurses has also been described and evaluated (Catalan *et al.* 1980*a,b*). The investigation took place in a psychiatric unit in a general hospital, where a multidisciplinary team of nurses, social workers, psychiatrists, and general practice trainees is involved in the psychiatric management of attempted suicide patients (Hawton *et al.* 1979). Doctors (psychiatric and general practice trainees) and nurses had been given special instruction in the assessment of deliberate self-poisoning patients. The adequacy of their assessment was investigated by having independent judges make ratings of transcripts from audio-tape recordings of their assessment interviews. The type of treatment offered, repetition of deliberate self-harm, and the attitudes of the patients and their general practitioners to the involvement of nurses were also examined. The study did not show any major differences between doctors and nurses, indicating that nurses who are specifically trained to assess attempted suicide patients and who work in a team where there is a psychiatrist available for consultation and supervision can be given responsibility for the initial assessment of these patients. A common factor in the two studies concerning assessment by non-medically qualified staff is that the social workers in the first study and the nurses in the second had a special interest in dealing with attempted suicide patients. Their enthusiasm for such work is likely to have played an important part in the results.

Another departure from the Hill Report recommendation on psychiatric assessment has been developed in Cambridge (Gardner *et al.* 1977, 1978). In a prospective randomized trial, Gardner and colleagues compared medical teams (junior physicians and general nurses) with psychiatrists in terms of the type of treatment recommended after assessment, the diagnoses made, and rates of further self-harm or suicide. The physicians and the nurses had been given instruction in the principles of psychiatric evaluation and there were regular meetings with a psychiatrist and psychiatric social worker during the trial. No differences between medical teams and psychiatrists were found, and the authors suggested that the official policy should be changed to allow physicians to decide in all cases whether a psychiatric opinion was required. The involvement of physicians in assessment is certainly an interesting development and one that requires further investigation in view of its possible limitations. However, the study was not designed in a way that would allow the conclusion that physicians were as accurate as psychiatrists in their diagnoses and recommendations. In addition, it is not known how easy it would be to apply these findings to other hospitals where psychiatric training is less adequate and there is a rapid turnover of junior medical staff. It is also uncertain whether already overworked physicians would welcome this development; the evidence from a survey of the views of doctors and nurses working in accident and emergency departments suggests that this would not be the case (Ghodse 1979). Physicians' attitudes to attempted suicide patients are to a large extent negative (Patel 1975; Ramon *et al.* 1975) and certainly less sympathetic than those of psychiatrists or nurses (Ramon *et al.* 1975; Hawton *et al.* 1981*b*). Nevertheless, this approach has been included in the Department of Health guidelines (DHSS 1984) with the recommendation that it is essential that each new intake of junior medical staff receives adequate psychiatric training in the assessment of attempted suicide patients, and that the physicians have regular access to psychiatrists to ensure that clinical standards are maintained.

The role of general practitioners in the assessment of deliberate self-poisoning has so far received very little attention. Although most patients who are brought to the attention of their doctors after an attempt are referred to hospital, a proportion are dealt with by general practitioners (p. 10). Presumably, this is more likely to happen when a small number of tablets is involved but the poor correlation between medical seriousness of an attempt and suicidal intent (Fox and Weissman 1975) would indicate that this practice should not be encouraged. On the other hand, the general practitioner's knowledge of the person's background and current circumstances could make him invaluable both in furthering the understanding of the attempt and in the provision of appropriate help. The Department of Health guidelines (1984) have recognized the involvement of the general practitioner in the assessment of patients who harm themselves, although the vagueness of its recommendations has been criticized (Kessel 1985). Before general practitioners are expected or encouraged to take on new duties their willingness to become more involved should be established, and easy access to experienced therapists for training and consultation should be available.

TREATMENT

Who should treat attempted suicide patients?

The management of patients who require psychiatric inpatient care after a suicide attempt remains the responsibility of psychiatrists, but recent work has shown the value of involving non-medical staff in treatment of those who do not require admission. Gibbons *et al.* (1978*a*) demonstrated that treatment by social workers using a standardized task-centred approach (Reid and Epstein 1972) was more effective in terms of improving patients' social problems than traditional care recommended by psychiatrists, although only for female patients (Gibbons 1979). In a study comparing outpatient with domiciliary treatment, non-medical therapists (one nurse and one social worker) were found to be as effective as psychiatrists (Hawton *et al.* 1981*a*). In a prospective, randomized trial, non-medical therapists (psychiatric nurses) have been found to be more effective than general practitioners in the management of female patients and patients with dyadic problems (Hawton *et al.* 1987). Other authors have reported the use of mental health workers and volunteers (Termansen and Bywater 1975), and nurses, social workers, and community workers (Welu 1977) as therapists. A conclusion that can be drawn from all these treatment studies is that when dealing with patients who do not require inpatient care, treatment by well-trained non-medical staff (social workers and nurses in· particular) is at least as effective as treatment given by psychiatrists. In the case of patients suffering from formal psychiatric disorder or requiring psychiatric inpatient treatment, the involvement of psychiatrists will continue to be necessary.

Where should patients be treated?

Patients requiring inpatient psychiatric care will usually be admitted to the psychiatric unit in the general hospital or to an acute bed in the local psychiatric hospital. Day-patient attendance can often be a very useful alternative, particularly when the patient is still experiencing serious difficulties in the absence of adequate support and when frequent contact is required. Day-patient care allows close monitoring of the patient's state while encouraging exploration and development of better ways of coping with problems, which can be enhanced with group therapy techniques (Temple and Catalan 1977).

In patients who do not need hospitalization, early intervention and easy access to the therapist can be provided using a flexible outpatient system, including direct telephone access. Involvement of the same therapist in assessment and follow-up is likely to increase attendance rates (Hawton *et al.* 1979). Routine domiciliary treatment does not seem justifiable, because of the expense and practical difficulties involved, but domiciliary treatment of selected cases, for example some working-class patients with marital problems, may be helpful.

TRAINING AND SUPERVISION

Staff involved in the psychiatric management of attempted suicide patients should receive appropriate training and supervision (DHSS 1984). These will have much in common with the kind of training that is given to therapists working in other settings, but should also include instruction relevant to the problems presented by attempted suicide patients.

Training in assessment of patients

During training, particular attention should be paid to psychosocial assessment in view of the nature of the act and potential problems associated with it, such as risk of suicide, risk of repetition, and presence of psychiatric disorder. This was dealt with fully in

Chapter 4. A therapist who undertakes the assessment of these patients should have sufficient factual knowledge about the problem of attempted suicide and should also have interviewing skills that allow him both to put patients at ease and obtain valid information. In our experience, instruction manuals and tutorials covering topics related to attempted suicide are an effective way of imparting factual information. Interviewing skills can be acquired and developed by placing individual trainees under the supervision of an experienced therapist who, over several weeks, monitors the trainee's progress. To begin with, the trainee sits in and observes the therapist's assessments; later their roles are reversed, so that the trainee can be given feedback about his performance. Audio-recordings of interviews can also be used to examine specific problems concerning communication between patient and trainee (Catalan *et al.* 1980*a*).

Supervision of therapists

After the initial period of training there should be adequate supervision by senior psychiatrists or other experienced therapists, preferably on a daily basis. New patients should be discussed in detail, particularly if the therapist is not medically qualified and there is a possibility of the patient suffering from psychiatric disorder. In hospitals where several therapists are involved in assessing patients, a daily meeting of those concerned and the psychiatrist can be the best form of providing supervision and psychiatric cover.

There should be opportunities for discussion of patients' sub-sequent management on a regular basis with experienced therapists. This can be accomplished by weekly or fortnightly review sessions, either with staff members individually, or in a group with other therapists. In addition to discussion of management problems, these sessions can be used to tackle some of the tensions and frustrations that can arise in teams of this kind, which are dealing with a rapid turnover of patients with acute problems, or problems that sometimes seem intractable, and where drop-out rates may be high.

CONCLUSIONS

There is no single, universally accepted type of service that is known to be more successful in the management of attempted suicide patients than any other. Local circumstances and availability of personnel and resources are likely to affect the organization of such services as much as any policy statement about the care of patients.

Poisoning Treatment Centres may have a special advantage (Kreitman 1980), but only one such centre currently exists and it is unlikely that more will be developed in the near future. Psychiatric units in general hospitals, on the other hand, are becoming a common feature, and here a multidisciplinary team of psychiatrists, psychiatric nurses, and social workers is very appropriate for the management of attempted suicide. In some hospitals, psychiatric staff and medical teams may develop a system of joint management like that described by Gardner and co-workers.

In hospitals without a psychiatric unit, the assessment of patients could be carried out by trained hospital staff, such as psychiatric nurses, social workers, and junior medical and psychiatric staff, under the supervision of a senior psychiatrist from the local psychiatric hospital, or by trained psychiatric nurses and social workers from the local psychiatric hospital working with psychiatrists, who would visit the hospital on a regular basis. Psychiatrists should continue to be involved in the assessment and management of these patients alongside other professionals. In addition, junior psychiatrists should be able to get adequate experience of the care of attempted suicide patients to improve their skills both in the management of patients with psychosocial problems and, in particular, the evaluation of suicide risk.

Whatever approach is adopted, it is clear that a comprehensive service for the management of attempted suicide patients should be staffed by personnel interested in working with such people and their problems. In addition, personnel working in this field must have received adequate training in the assessment procedure, and in the management of interpersonal and family problems. Instruction manuals, tape-recordings of assessment intervies, and interviews carried out under the supervision of experienced therapists over several weeks could be used for the training of new therapists. Adequate supervision by senior psychiatrists should be available, preferably through daily meetings where all referrals can be discussed before discharge from hospital. Similarly, staff should be able to discuss their subsequent management regularly with an experienced supervisor (Black and Pond 1980).

A good service may cost more in terms of staffing, but would contribute to a reduction in medical-bed occupancy by providing early assessment. It would also lead to a better use of the skills of social workers, psychiatric nurses, physicians, and psychiatrists. Finally, it would be more likely to promote positive changes in the quality of life of patients and their families.

10

Prevention of attempted suicide

INTRODUCTION

Suicide attempters are usually experiencing considerable personal unhappiness and social difficulties which often improve after their attempts (p. 46). However, no one has seriously challenged the view that attempted suicide should be regarded as an inappropriate way of coping with problems. This is not only because of the risks to the health of the attempters and the distress to families and friends, but also because of the implications for the health services in terms of use of limited resources. For all these reasons, it is clear that attempted suicide should be discouraged as a way of coping.

In this chapter, preventive measures will be discussed and examined, first with regard to *primary prevention*, or preventive work aimed at people who have not yet attempted suicide, and then in terms of *secondary prevention*, or prevention of further episodes of self-poisoning or self-injury. It could be argued that the best way of dealing with attempted suicide would be to prevent its occurrence in the first place; but this is not an easy task, and one that often extends beyond the reach of the clinician. Secondary prevention, on the other hand, should always be a concern of the therapist involved in the management of patients who have already made attempts.

PRIMARY PREVENTION

There is no single and all-important cause of attempted suicide. On the contrary, a variety of interpersonal, social, and psychological factors may contribute to it. As discussed in Chapter 3, a good deal is known about the circumstances associated with suicide attempts. For example, it is known that attempts usually follow acute and serious interpersonal conflict, that chronic difficulties and social problems are common, and that a large proportion of patients have taken steps to gain help from their family doctors before the attempt. The diversity of factors and problems suggests that no single preventive measure is likely to be relevant to all patients, and that effective prevention will have to include different procedures at the various stages in the chain of events leading up to the suicide attempt.

There are several measures which might reduce the chances of a suicide attempt in an individual at risk. These include making available emergency access to help, identification and adequate management by health and social agencies of those at risk, control of the means used to cause self-harm, modification of public attitudes to coping with problems in general and attempted suicide in particular, and measures aimed at improving the material and social circumstances of the population at risk.

Provision of services offering immediate help to potential attempters

The Samaritans in this country and the Suicide Prevention Centres in the United States are examples of emergency services providing 24-hour telephone access and other facilities for patients at risk of completed suicide. However, no services have been developed explicitly for the prevention of *suicide attempts*. Evidence of the efficacy of the Samaritans in reducing suicide mortality is contradictory. Bagley (1968) found a fall in the rate of suicide in cities with a Samaritan branch when compared with matched cities without Samaritans, where suicide rates increased. However, replication of the study, including matched control cities selected by three different methods, failed to show any differences (Jennings *et al.* 1978).

In the United States, three studies have failed to demonstrate any reduction in suicide rates with the development of Suicide Prevention Centres (Weiner 1969; Lester 1974; Bridge *et al.* 1977). However, in a recent study a substantial decline in suicide rates among young white females (under 25 years of age) was found in areas in which crisis centres were established, compared with a considerable increase in those in which such developments had not taken place (Miller *et al.* 1984). Young white females are by far the most common users of crisis and suicide prevention facilities, and so these findings support the possibility that crisis centres do have a preventive effect.

The stated aim of these programmes is to prevent suicide. It is doubtful, however, whether they would prevent attempted suicide. Holding (1974) monitored the numbers of suicide attempters admitted to the Edinburgh Poisoning Treatment Centre in the weeks before, during, and after the screening of an 11-episode weekly television programme illustrating the work of the Samaritans. While there was a marked increase in referrals to the Samaritans during and after the showing of the series, there was no change in the number of suicide attempts during the relevant periods. These results are consistent with the findings of Chowdhury and Kreitman (1971), and Kreitman and Chowdhury (1973a), who found attempted suicide patients and Samaritan clients to be different in many respects—the Samaritan clients, for example, including a greater proportion of men, and more socially isolated individuals.

It has been shown that most suicide attempters are aware of the existence of agencies where they could obtain help, such as the general practitioner, social workers, or the Samaritans (Kreitman and Chowdhury 1973b); in fact, a significant proportion of attempters had been in touch with one or more of these agencies in the weeks preceding the attempt (Bancroft *et al.* 1977). Despite this, they had not used these potential sources of help instead of taking an overdose or injuring themselves. Kreitman and Chowdhury (1973b) found that the most common reason given for not getting in touch with a helping agency was that the overdose was seen as a way of relieving strain or going to sleep. Other reasons commonly given included criticism of the services, that the problems were too personal for discussion, and that the person wanted to die. A proportion of patients admitted the overdose was aimed at influencing a partner or other person in close proximity. These findings suggest that, at the time of the act, helping agencies were regarded as irrelevant to what the person wanted to achieve, or unhelpful on the basis of previous experience of them. Nevertheless, Bancroft *et al.* (1977) found that more than half the attempters felt they had needed some form of help before the act, and that the most common type of help wanted was someone to talk to.

The overall impression resulting from these findings is that emergency services specifically designed for potential attempters might be of benefit to some, but the impulsive nature of the act, and the fact that the attempt often appears to be carried out with a particular purpose not related to help-seeking, but aimed at someone in close proximity, reduces the chances of preventing suicide attempts by this method alone. More success might be expected from measures directed towards offering help at an earlier stage when the patient is less distressed, for example when the patient gets in touch with the general practitioner.

Identification and adequate management of people at risk

It would be reasonable to expect that the extension and development of community psychiatric services would lead to a reduction in the rate of suicide and attempted suicide, but there is little evidence that this is so. Walk (1967) suggested that the introduction of a community psychiatric service in Chichester may have reduced the suicide rate in elderly female patients. However, Nielsen and Videbech (1973) failed to find any effect on the suicide rate of the introduction of a community service to an island population. Koller and Slaghuis (1978) mentioned the development of community health centres in Hobart, Tasmania, at the time when the rates of attempted suicide were decreasing, but did not indicate any causal connection. One interesting example of community-based services is the Craigmillar experiment in Edinburgh described by Ebie (1971). The Health, Welfare, and Advice Centre was established to co-ordinate the work of a variety of voluntary agencies and statutory social services in an area characterized by severe social problems and high rates of attempted suicide. The Centre was very popular and attracted many people with similar demographic characteristics, including marital and social difficulties, to those who attempt suicide. The suicide attempt rates, however, remained essentially unchanged, although in other areas the rates of suicide attempts continued to increase (Kreitman 1977). This finding is encouraging, but the results should be interpreted with caution as the control areas were not matched in terms of the pre-existing levels of social problems and attempted suicide.

The general practitioner has a potentially important role in the prevention of attempted suicide. The high proportion of suicide attempters who visit their general practitioners not long before making attempts has already been noted (Chapter 3). Hawton and Blackstock (1976) found that during these visits the doctors had, in most cases, detected symptoms of psychological distress, including anxiety and depression, and were also aware that the patients were contending with social and relationship difficulties. However, the majority of patients were prescribed psychotropic medication; this was often the very same medication that was used in the subsequent overdoses.

Of course, it should not be assumed that prescribing of psychotropic medication for such problems actually *causes* patients to take overdoses. It is in fact possible that some patients, especially those with marked symptoms of anxiety or depression, benefit from drugs and are better able to cope with their problems as a result, but the size of this group is not known. However, it can be argued that prescribing of psychotropic drugs when marital and social difficulties are pre-eminent might encourage the patient to believe that such problems are due to 'illness' and therefore not surmountable by his own efforts. He may feel that his doctor has prematurely terminated his assessment of his problems, thereby increasing his sense of helplessness and discouraging further discussion with the doctor. Finally, it might reinforce the notion that taking tablets is the way to deal with stress, and it also provides the means of taking an overdose. Patients have been known to report that the idea of taking an overdose had not crystallized in their minds until they received a prescription from their doctor. Minor tranquillizers, in particular, have been the subject of much criticism in view of the extent of their prescribing in general practice, their doubtful efficacy and the risks associated with their use (Catalan and Gath 1985). There is evidence that brief counselling by the general practitioner can be as effective as minor tranquillizers for patients with mild to moderate symptoms of anxiety and depression associated with social difficulties, without the risks involved in the use of minor tranquillizers. Brief counselling, consisting of exploration of symptoms and social difficulties, reassurance and advice, need not be time-consuming and is generally more acceptable to patients than psychotropic drugs (Catalan *et al.* 1984*a,b*).

Although many patients are prescribed psychotropic medication, only a small proportion of these will go on to take an overdose. Therefore, it is important to try to identify the factors which might assist general practitioners to recognize those patients who are at special risk of attempted suicide. In a prospective study of general practice prescribing involving more than 40 000 people over a 2-

year period, Skegg *et al.* (1983) found that only three in a thousand of those who had received psychotropics went on to take an overdose of the drugs within the following 12 months. The highest rates of self-poisoning were among those who received anti-depressants and minor tranquillizers. Women were found to be more likely than men to poison themselves after receiving psychotropics, and patients aged between 15 and 29 years had the highest rates. These findings are consistent with the epidemiological evidence available (Chapter 2), and could assist general practitioners to identify individuals at risk.

It is also well recognized that overdoses are often associated with threatened or actual disruption of a marital relationship, or a relationship with a boyfriend or girlfriend. Parents (especially mothers) who have such poor relationships with their children that abuse or neglect are suspected are also at special risk. It has been suggested that the presence of feelings of *hopelessness* may be a more sensitive indicator of attempted suicide risk than depression itself (Minkoff *et al.* 1973, Beck *et al.* 1975a,b). Therefore, the doctor should ask the patient about his feelings about the future and his ability to cope. The danger of attempted suicide among patients with epilepsy, especially males, has already been discussed. A history of alcohol abuse or a tendency to impulsive behaviour should also alert the doctor. These are some factors to be taken into account; clearly, further work is needed to identify other risk factors which might alert the general practitioner to the possibility of an attempt. Knowledge of such factors is important because if a doctor is worried that a certain patient is likely to take an overdose, it would be better to explore the patient's difficulties and share this anxiety with the patient instead of avoiding discussing the issue or prescribing psychotropic drugs.

When patients who did not contact their general practitioners before their attempts were questioned about why they had not gone to their doctor, it was found that many were reluctant to trouble him, some had found him unhelpful in the past, and others thought he was unlikely to be helpful or might even be unsympathetic (Hawton and Blackstock 1976). This suggests that patients might be discouraged from taking overdoses if their general practitioners were seen as more willing to discuss psychological and social difficulties, or if other mental health professionals were available in health centres.

Recognition of those individuals likely to make attempts is only part of the process of prevention. This would have to be followed up by provision of appropriate help. Some general practitioners may be willing to offer individual counselling or marital therapy themselves. Others might prefer to refer patients to special agencies for such help, including social workers, counsellors attached to practices, marriage guidance counsellors, and so on. Because of the immediate nature of such patients' problems it is important that whatever form of help is offered should be available without too much delay, and for this reason health-centre-based therapists may be of particular value, as has been shown in the case of psychologists (Robson *et al.* 1984) and social workers (Shepherd *et al.* 1979).

This does not mean that psychtropic drugs have no role in the treatment of patients who might attempt suicide. However, they should be prescribed only where there are definite indications. Thus, antidepressants should be prescribed in adequate therapeutic doses (Johnson 1973) where there is clear evidence of underlying depressive illness, not where depression seems to be entirely symptomatic of social problems. Tranquillizers should be prescribed only for short periods to help patients through crises where their levels of anxiety are such that their coping ability is grossly impaired. Such patients are uncommon in general practice; they are more likely to be seen in psychiatric outpatient clinics. Hypnotics should be prescribed, preferably for short periods only, where insomnia secondary to distress is undermining an individual's resources, such as during a severe grief reaction. The role of psychotropic medication in such cases should be made clear to the patient, particularly where medication is only a means of assisting coping behaviour rather than dealing with patients' fundamental problems. Automatic prescribing of psychotropic drugs, which commonly occurs (Freed 1976), should be avoided. Many suicide attempters are known to receive repeat prescriptions for psychotropic drugs from their general practitioners, often including combinations of several drugs (Prescott and Highly 1985). This group of patients should be reviewed periodically to establish whether medication is indicated or whether alternative approaches should be used.

Better control of drugs, toxic preparations, and firearms

About 60 per cent of self-poisoners take psychotropic drugs that have been prescribed for them in their overdoses (Hawton *et al.* 1977). The pattern of self-poisoning with prescribed drugs largely reflects general prescribing patterns of psychotropic medication. This was borne out very clearly in the parallel decline in barbiturate prescribing, and both non-fatal overdoses (Barraclough 1976) and suicides (Jones 1977). On the other hand, psychotropic drugs such as minor tranquillizers and antidepressants are now being prescribed on a large scale by general practitioners (Skegg *et al.* 1977), and this probably contributed to some extent to the increase in overdoses of these substances. Opinions vary as to whether more cautious and rational use of these drugs by general practitioners leading to a reduction in prescribing of tranquillizers and antidepressants would result in a decline in the number of suicide attempts (Kreitman 1977). A positive correlation has indeed been reported between the number of prescriptions for psychotropic drugs issued by general practitioners in England and Wales and the rate of deliberate self-poisoning, and it has been estimated that a reduction of 1000 psychotropic prescriptions would be associated with 3.8 fewer admissions as a result of deliberate self-poisoning (Forster and Frost 1985). The introduction in 1985 of a restricted list of preparations available on the NHS in the United Kingdom, if accompanied by a drop in the number of prescriptions for psychotropic drugs, may have an affect on the rates of self-poisoning with such drugs. However, making prescribed drugs less easily available is unlikely to help most patients unless it is accompanied by discussion of their problems or referral to appropriate agencies. It could indeed be argued that if adequate counselling is not provided some of these patients might then turn to potentially more dangerous drugs such as aspirin or paracetamol and use them in overdoses.

More than one-third of self-poisoners use preparations which can be bought over the counter (Proudfoot and Park 1978). Control of the availability of non-prescribed drugs might therefore be another means of prevention. This is a complex problem. Overdoses of these drugs are most common among teenagers (Hawton and Goldacre 1982), who are less likely than adults to have visited their general practitioner before the attempt (Hawton and Blackstock 1976). In these cases, prevention might have to be in terms of limiting sales from chemist shops. Kessel (1965) has suggested a limit to the amount of tablets that could be dispensed at a given time, and in some areas chemist shop assistants are instructed to refer customers to senior staff when large amounts of tablets are being requested. The use of special blister packaging of tablets or individual wrapping in foil to delay their ingestion in the case of impulsive overdoses has also been suggested (Fox 1975). General health education about the toxic and long-term effects of drugs could also be relevant here. Gazzard *et al.* (1976) used a questionnaire to ask patients who had taken overdoses of paracetamol about their knowledge of the effects of this substance and found that only 11 per cent knew about the possibility of severe hepatic complications that can occur after an interval of several days. None of the patients interviews said they would have taken paracetamol had they been aware of this danger. The information was collected after the attempt and it is not clear whether patients would have acted as they claimed they would but, taken at face value, the findings support the case for better health education and warning about the effects of drugs.

It has been suggested that educating people to keep a minimum of tablets in the home would help to reduce the risk of impulsive overdoses (Kessel 1965). One survey showed that most households contain prescribed medicines, but that these drugs are used regularly in only half of the cases (Leach and White 1978). The most commonly found types of medication were drugs acting on the central nervous system. These findings lend support to the view that persuading people to dispose of unused or rarely used medicines stored in the home might play a part in reducing the numbers of impulsive overdoses of these substances.

In the United States, concern has been expressed about the contribution of firearms to suicide. As noted earlier, (p. 17), between 1953 and 1978 the age-adjusted rate of suicide by means of firearms increased from 4.9 to 7.1 per 100 000 population, while rates for other methods remained unchanged (Boyd 1983). There is also evidence that the suicide rates found in different States are associated with the strictness of the gun control laws (Lester and Murrell 1980). It would therefore seem sensible to conclude that greater control over the availability and sale of firearms would make an important contribution to the prevention of suicidal behaviour.

Modification of public attitudes and education concerning life crises

Attempted suicide appears to have become an acceptable way of expressing distress among some people, and has therefore been likened to a fashion. The use of propaganda to make this behaviour unfashionable again has been suggested (Stanley 1969), but no health education programme has ever been put forward to this purpose and it is difficult to know whether such an approach would be feasible. One possible drawback could be that some people might decide to take an overdose as a result of learning about it through the media or public discussion, even if the behaviour had been presented as an inappropriate way of coping.

It is reasonable to expect that public attitudes and beliefs about attempted suicide will affect its incidence. Sale *et al.* (1975) interviewed a random general population sample of females over the age of 15 in Hobart, Tasmania, and found that overdoses and self-injuries were regarded as potentially lethal in most cases. In addition, suicide attempts were usually regarded as implying a wish to die and the existence of mental illness, while less acceptable reasons, such as manipulation of others, were infrequently considered. One interesting finding was that people who reported personal contact with suicide attempters were more likely to have hostile attitudes towards attempted suicide. This would suggest that a spontaneous decline in the incidence of attempted suicide might be expected as greater numbers of people come into personal contact with someone who has attempted suicide and public attitudes towards attempters become more negative. Sale *et al.* (1975) have suggested that increased public education about the facts of attempted suicide, as opposed to commonly held beliefs, might contribute to the development of less favourable attitudes, which in turn might lead to a reduction in suicide attempts.

The use of educational programmes for schoolchildren and adolescents to develop their ability to deal with problems and rehearse future ways of coping have also been advocated (Morgan 1979).

In the United States, imaginative programmes have been developed to heighten the awareness of teachers and pupils in relation to adolescent suicide, with the objective of preventing it (Ross 1986; Ryerson 1986). Such an approach is of considerable interest, although there are many methodological problems involved in establishing its efficacy.

Improvement in material and social circumstances

The knowledge that attempted suicide is more common among those of lower socioeconomic status and in socially deprived areas, and that attempts often occur against the background of financial and employment problems, suggests that prevention will to some extent depend on political and social factors. Measures directly towards the amelioration of these conditions might be expected to contribute to the prevention of attempted suicide, although other factors—such as the availability of drugs, cultural attitudes, and the level of services available—might have a more immediate effect.

SECONDARY PREVENTION

The obvious meaning of secondary prevention in relation to attempted suicide is reduction in the likelihood of further attempts. In addition, secondary prevention could also be applied to the alleviation of social and psychological difficulties which might lead to attempts. Naturally, one would assume that these two aspects of secondary prevention go hand in hand. It is surprising, therefore, to find that there is often a disjunction between the two (Kreitman 1979). Thus, prospective studies concerning different forms of treatment have demonstrated benefits for social and psychological functioning, but not for repetition rates. Such studies are discussed below.

Retrospective investigations of the effectiveness of psychiatric help for attempted suicide patients have provided encouraging results, but the drawbacks of retrospective research, including poor matching of comparison groups especially with regard to subtle factors like motivation for treatment, cast doubts on the validity of the findings. In the first of these studies, Greer and Bagley (1971) found after an 18-month follow-up that patients who had received no psychiatric attention before discharge from hospital after attempts repeated more often (39 per cent) than those who had received either brief psychiatric contact (26 per cent repeated) or more prolonged psychiatric contact (20 per cent repeated). These findings persisted when variables found to correlate with repetition were controlled for across the three groups. In a second study, Kennedy (1972) found that repetition after 1 year was less common in patients admitted to the Edinburgh Regional Poisoning Treatment Centre (12 per cent) than in those who made attempts and were not referred to the Centre, irrespective of whether the latter were referred to psychiatrists elsewhere (38 per cent repeated) or not (37 per cent repeated). Patients admitted to the Centre received prompt assessment and, where indicated, psychiatric aftercare (Kreitman 1977). When the groups were matched for those with and without a history of previous attempts, the difference between patients admitted to the Centre and those who were not persisted. Unfortunately, these encouraging results have not been substantiated in prospective studies of special forms of treatment, although it is worth noting that no proper, prospective controlled study in which patients have been randomly assigned to either a treatment or a no-treatment group has been carried out. This is probably because of the ethical and practical considerations.

Prospective studies of intervention have been confined mostly to comparison of one form of treatment with another. Chowdhury *et al.* (1973) in Edinburgh concentrated on patients who had already made repeat attempts. A special aftercare service was set up—staffed by psychiatrists and social workers—which consisted of weekly outpatient clinics, domiciliary visiting where necessary, and an emergency call service. Efforts were made to contact patients who did not keep appointments. Patients allocated to normal care were given outpatient appointments to see a psychiatrist or social worker, but non-attenders were not pursued. After 6 months no significant difference was found between repetition rates of patients in the experimental group (24 per cent) and those who received normal care (23 per cent). However, patients in the experimental group, particularly the women, did show significantly greater improvements in their social circumstances (finance, housing, and employment) than those allocated to conventional care.

Similar results were obtained in a study of social work intervention in Southampton (Gibbons *et al.* 1978*a*). The experimental service in this study consisted of task-centred casework (Reid and Epstein 1972) provided by social workers. Task-centred casework is similar to the brief problem-orientated approach to treatment .described in Chapter 5. No difference between the repetition rates of patients offered this service and those who received conventional care was detected at the one-year follow-up. However, when interviewed at a 4-month follow-up, more of the experimental group showed overall improvement in their social problems (70 per cent) than the control group (53 per cent). Also, more of the former were satisfied with the service they had received. Again, the benefits of the experimental service were confined to women (Gibbons 1979).

In a study in Oxford the effectiveness of home-based treatment was compared with treatment of outpatients (Hawton *et al.* 1981*a*). There were two medical and two non-medical therapists. Although domiciliary treatment was far more acceptable to patients in that many more offered this form of care kept their appointments, no difference was found in outcome between the two forms of treatment in terms either of repetition or measures of psychological distress and social functioning. The treatment approach used in both conditions was the brief problem-orientated therapy described in Chapter 5. Three-quarters of the patients who completed treatment found it helpful. They particularly appreciated the problem-orientated nature of the approach.

In a large-scale Swedish study of intervention with self-poisoners, patients in one group were offered psychiatric, social, and psychological help whereas another group was offered traditional care (Ettlinger 1975). No differences in terms of further attempts or of completed suicide were found between the two groups after a 5-year follow-up. Nor were differences found when crude measures of social functioning was examined. Unfortunately, this study suffered from not being a properly controlled trial. In addition, the care offered to the special treatment group was not at all intensive.

A second Oxford study compared out-patient counselling, using the same brief problem-orientated approach described in Chapter 5, with routine care given by the general practitioner (Hawton *et al.* 1987). Although no differences were found between patients in the two treatment conditions in terms of their subsequent psychological and social adjustment and repetition rates, two categories of patients, women and patients of either sex with dyadic problems, showed significant improvement when given outpatient counselling.

There is only one reported example of successful prevention of repetition of further attempts. In a double-blind placebo controlled trial, intramuscular flupenthixol was effective in reducing the number of further attempts in a small group of patients with a history of two or more episodes (Montgomery *et al.* 1979). This interesting and surprising result awaits replication. Liberman and Eckman (1981) compared the effects of behaviour therapy and insight-oriented therapy in the inpatient treatment of patients with a history of at least two recent attempts. Patients in both treatment groups made significantly less attempts after treatment than in the two years before the study, but the lack of an untreated control group means that the efficacy of the treatments in preventing further attempts remains open to question. However, behaviour therapy was more effective than insight-oriented therapy for patients' subsequent depression, anxiety, and assertiveness.

In summary, therefore, most special aftercare services have had no effect on repetition rates after attempted suicide. There is, however, evidence that they can benefit patients' social and psychological problems, but that these benefits are confined to women and people with problems in their relationships with their partners (most of whom are women). At present we seem able to do little to help male attempters by means of counselling approaches. This may be because they generally suffer more serious problems, often complicated by personality difficulties and alcohol abuse.

None of the studies described above have been concerned with patients suffering from serious psychiatric illness or being at immediate risk of suicide. Usually, such patients are admitted to psychiatric inpatient care (see Chapter 7). Few clinicians would doubt that the care offered to these patients is effective.

CONCLUSIONS

Primary prevention of suicide attempts is extremely difficult and continues to present a challenge to health and social services alike. Several possible methods of prevention have been discussed in this chapter, including emergency services, community-based counselling facilities, identification and adequate management by general practitioners of people at risk, rational prescribing of psychotropic drugs and control of toxic preparations and firearms, and educational measures. Further evaluation of these and development of other approaches is required. Similarly, the prevention of further episodes of self-poisoning or self-injury continues to be a problem, and while retrospective investigations have given support to the policy of psychiatric intervention, prospective studies have failed to demonstrate any effect on repetition rates. However, treatment studies show that special forms of treatment can have a positive effect on the psychological and social functioning of many patients, especially women.

11

Concluding comments

Attempted suicide continues to present a very challenging problem for medical and psychiatric services. The increase in the extent of the behaviour during the 1970s had a considerable effect on medical teams, psychiatrists, social workers, and general practitioners. The response to the problem has been variable, with excellent services being established in some areas and woefully inadequate facilities continuing in others. It is hoped that discussion of the problems faced by attempted suicide patients and the factors which should be kept in mind during their assessment will have left the reader in no doubt as to the crucial nature of the assessment procedure for such patients and the need for it to be done in a careful way by staff who have been appropriately trained.

Consideration of the diversity of difficulties that face attempted suicide patients, and the range of both the degree of suicidal intent and risk of repetition associated with their behaviour, should have demonstrated why it is most important that the facilities available for management of these patients must be flexible and allow a variety of options. There must always be an opportunity for psychiatric inpatient care when required. However, it is likely that well under 10 per cent of patients will need to be admitted to a psychiatric unit provided that other treatment facilities are available. For many patients, brief problem-orientated outpatient care seems to be a very satisfactory means of helping them tackle the difficulties. This does not demand a high degree of psychotherapeutic experience, but does require a good deal of common-sense. In a few cases home-based treatment using the same approach may be helpful, although large-scale use of domiciliary treatment does not appear to be justified. Not all patients require specialized help after an attempt. A substantial proportion can be referred back to their general practitioners once a thorough assessment has been carried out. The general practitioner may wish to provide his own aftercare for some patients. It is extremely important that there should be good liaison between the hospital-based service and the primary care team.

During the past few years a number of different models for hospital services for attempted suicide patients have been developed. Our experience of a multidisciplinary team approach, in which psychiatrists, nursing staff, and social workers all play a prominent role, has been very encouraging. As indicated in the recent guidelines of the Department of Health and Social Security (1984), a sensible approach towards establishing comprehensive services would be for clinicians in each area to set up a service which most suits local conditions and needs. Whatever type of service is developed, the most important factors would appear to be that, first, the members of a service should be enthusiastic about dealing with attempted suicide patients; secondly, they should receive appropriate training in assessment and management; and thirdly, supervision by experienced staff should be available.

Staff working in centres in which facilities for attempted suicide patients are developed should endeavour to monitor trends in the behaviour in their area. This need not demand a large-scale research effort, but a simple record of all hospital admissions for self-poisoning and self-injury. Such monitoring might help provide feedback to the service on its effectiveness. However, the main use would be to identify groups of patients to whom special attention should be paid because of changing patterns of self-poisoning and self-injury in the area.

There are a number of other needs associated with the problem of attempted suicide. Apart from a general improvement in clinical services, further research is required to evaluate the effectiveness of different methods of managing patients after they have left hospital. In particular, more still needs to be known about the characteristics of patients most likely to benefit from treatment. We now know that special aftercare can benefit women, but male attempters appear more difficult to help. Further work is required to find new therapeutic methods for men. Child and adolescent attempters are a group with special requirements, and careful thought should be given to how best to meet their needs. Guidelines have been published in the UK concerning the management of attempters under the age of 16 (Bulletin of the Royal College of Psychiatrists 1982). These recommend that a local child psychiatric team should be involved with all such individuals and their families, and that young people up to 14 years of age should be admitted to a paediatric ward, rather than a general medical or surgical ward. The general hospital psychiatric team should be able to provide assessment of older adolescents; one member of the team might take a particular interest in this age group. In some cases, especially those with serious psychiatric disorders, the local adolescent psychiatric service should be involved as early as possible. In others, the general hospital psychiatric service will be able to provide aftercare, including where necessary, family therapy.

Individuals who repeatedly take overdoses or injure themselves constitute a group for which there is a considerable dearth of information, both of the causes of this behaviour and means of providing effective help. Chronic repeaters therefore should be the focus of intensive research aimed, first, at describing their difficulties and the reasons for the behaviour, and secondly, at evaluation of different methods of management, including the possible role of medication.

We appear to be a long way from finding effective means of primary prevention of attempted suicide. At present it seems likely that the most hopeful approaches rest in three areas. The first is the limitation in prescribing of psychotropic drugs and the provision of alternative forms of help for individuals with symptoms of depression and anxiety secondary to social problems. This approach would have to be aimed primarily at general practice. Already there have been a number of reports of developments of this kind. For example, brief counselling by general practitioners has been shown to be as effective as benzodioazepine tranquillizers for patients with minor affective disorders of recent onset (Catalan *et al.* 1984*b*). Encouraging experiments have been carried out utilizing the special skills of social workers (Cooper *et al.* 1974; Shepherd *et al.* 1979), clinical psychologists (Johnston 1978; Robson *et al.* 1984), and marriage guidance counsellors (Marsh and Barr 1975; Cohen and Halpern 1978) working in general practice to provide help for patients with social problems.

The second approach to prevention is the implementation of educational programmes aimed at modifying the attitudes of young people to attempted suicide. This requires very careful planning to avoid any risk of encouraging the behaviour. Our knowledge of deliberate self-poisoning in young people indicates that such measures could be largely confined to girls.

The third approach to prevention, and the most difficult, lies in economic and social changes which could lead to general improvements in standards of living. Unfortunately, current trends, especially with regard to unemployment, are in the opposite direction.

We hope that primary prevention of attempted suicide will not continue to be solely a focus for conjecture. Apart from the load attempted suicide places on health service facilities, it is not yet known whether the high levels of the behaviour in recent years will subsequently be reflected in an increase in the numbers of completed suicides. This would certainly occur if the rates of suicides among those who make attempts continue at the levels mentioned earlier (p. 21).

The needs associated with the problem of attempted suicide are clearly both considerable and pressing. It is to be hoped that the interest in these patients, which has led to an impressive research effort and also the establishment of specialized clinical services, will continue despite the major economic strictures which now face the Health Service.

Recommended reading

Ewing, C. P. (1978). *Crisis intervention as psychotherapy*. Oxford University Press, New York.

Farmer, R. and Hirsch, S. (1980). *The suicide syndrome*. Croom Helm, London.

Hawton, K. (1986). *Suicide and attempted suicide among children and adolescants*. Sage, Beverly Hills.

Kreitman, N. (1977). *Parasuicide*. Wiley, London.

McCulloch, J. W. and Philip, A. E. (1972). *Suicidal behaviour*. Pergamon, Oxford.

Morgan, H. G. (1979). *Death wishes? The understanding and management of deliberate self-harm*. Wiley, Chichester.

References

Aitken, R. C. B., Buglass, D., and Kreitman, N. (1969). The changing pattern of attempted suicide in Edinburgh, 1962–67. *British Journal of preventive and social Medicine* 23, 111–15.

Alderson, M. R. (1974). Self-poisoning: what is the future? *Lancet i*, 1040–3.

Bagley, C. R. (1968). The evaluation of a suicide prevention scheme by an ecological method. *Social Science and Medicine* 2, 1–14.

Bancroft, J. (1979). Crisis intervention. In *An introduction to the psychotherapies* (ed. S. Bloch) pp. 83–101. Oxford University Press, Oxford.

——, Hawton, K., Simkin, S., Kingston, B., Cumming, C., and Whitwell, D. (1979). The reasons people give for taking overdoses: a further enquiry. *British Journal of medical Psychology* 52, 353–65.

—— and Marsack, P. (1977). The repetitiveness of self-poisoning and self-injury. *British Journal of Psychiatry* 131, 394–9.

——, Skrimshire, A., Casson, J., Harvard-Watts, O., and Reynolds, F. (1977). People who deliberately poison or injure themselves: their problems and their contacts with helping agencies. *Psychological Medicine* 7, 289–303.

——,——, Reynolds, F., Simkin, S., and Smith, J. (1975). Self-poisoning and self-injury in the Oxford area: epidemiological aspects 1969–73. *British Journal of preventive and social Medicine* 29, 170–7.

Barnes, R. A. (1979). Characteristics of the chronic suicide attempter. In *Proceedings communication: 10th International congress for suicide prevention and crisis intervention, Ottawa,* 17–20 June, 1979.

Barraclough, B. (1972). Suicide prevention, recurrent affective disorder and lithium. *British Journal of Psychiatry* 121, 391–2.

—— (1976). Barbiturate prescribing: psychiatrists' views. *British medical Journal* ii, 927–8.

——, Bunch, J., Nelson, B., and Sainsbury, P. (1974). A hundred cases of suicide: clinical aspects. *British Journal of Psychiatry* 125, 355–73.

Beck, A. T., Beck, R., and Kovacs, M. (1975a). Classification of suicidal behaviours: I. Quantifying intent and medical lethality. *American Journal of Psychiatry* 132, 285–7.

—— and Emery, G. (1985). *Anxiety disorders and phobias*. Basic Books, New York.

——, Kovacs, M., and Weissman, A. (1975*b*). Hopelessness and suicidal behaviour: an overview. *Journal of the American medical Association* **234**, 1146–9.

——, Rush, A. J., Shaw, B. F., and Emery, G. (1979). *Cognitive therapy of depression*. Guilford, New York.

——, Schuyler, D., and Herman, J. (1974*a*). Development of suicidal intent scales. In *The prediction of suicide* (ed. A. T. Beck, H. L. P. Resnik, and D. J. Lettieri). Charles Press, Maryland.

——, Steer, R. A., Kovacs, M., and Garrison, B. (1985). Hopelessness and eventual suicide: a 10 year prospective study of patients hospitalized with suicidal ideation. *American Journal of Psychiatry* **145**, 559–63.

——, Weissman, A., Lester, D., and Trexler, L. (1974*b*). The measurement of pessimism: the Hopelessness Scale. *Journal of consulting and clinical Psychology* **42**, 861–5.

Bell, A. P. and Weinberg, M. S. (1978). *Homosexualities: a study of diversity among men and women*. Mitchell Beazley, London.

Bergstrand, C. G. and Otto, U. (1962). Suicidal attempts in adolescence and childhood. *Acta Paediatrica* **51**, 17–26.

Birtchnell, J. and Floyd, S. (1974). Attempted suicide and the menstrual cycle—a negative conclusion. *Journal of psychosomatic Research* **18**, 361–9.

—— and —— (1975). Further menstrual characteristics of suicide attempters. *Journal of psychosomatic Research* **19**, 81–5.

Black, D. and Pond, D. (1980). Management of patients after self-poisoning. *British medical Journal* **281**, 1141.

Bloch, S. and Chodoff, P. (eds.) (1981). *Psychiatric ethics*. Oxford University Press.

Boyd, J. H. (1983). The increasing rate of suicide by firearms. *New England Journal of Medicine* **308**, 872–4.

Brandon, S. (1970). Crisis theory and possibilities of therapeutic intervention. *British Journal of Psychiatry* **117**, 627–33.

——, Cowley, P., McDonald, D., Neville, P., Palmer, R., and Wellstood-Eason, S. (1984). Electroconvulsive therapy: results in depressive illness from the Leicestershire trial. *British medical Journal* **288**, 22–5.

Brewer, C. and Farmer, R. (1985). Self-poisoning in 1984: a prediction that didn't come true. *British medical Journal* **290**, 391.

Bridge, T. P., Potkin, S. G., Zung, W. W. K., and Soldo. B. J. (1977). Suicide prevention centres: ecological study of effectiveness. *Journal of nervous and mental Diseases* **164**, 18–24.

Buckle, R. C., Linnane, J., and McConachy, N. (1965). Attempted suicide presenting at the Alfred Hospital, Melbourne. *Medical Journal of Australia* **i**, 754–8.

Buglass, D. and Horton, J. (1974). A scale for predicting subsequent suicidal behaviour. *British Journal of Psychiatry* **124**, 573–8.

—— and McCulloch, J. W. (1970). Further suicidal behaviour: the development and validation of predictive scales. *British Journal of Psychiatry* **116**, 483–91.

Bulletin of the Royal College of Psychiatrists (1982). The management of parasuicide in young people under sixteen. *Bulletin of the Royal College of Psychiatrists* **6**, 182–5.

Caplan, G. (1964). *Principles of preventive psychiatry*. Basic Books, New York.

Carpenter, R. G. (1959). Statistical analysis of suicide and other mortality rates of students. *British Journal of preventive and social Medicine* **13**, 163–74.

Catalan, J. (1983). Attempted suicide and homosexuality. *British Journal of sexual Medicine* **20**, 11–14.

—— and Gath D. H. (1985). Benzodiazepines in general practice: time for a decision. *British medical Journal* **290**, 1374–6.

——, ——, Bond, A., and Martin, P. (1984*a*). The effects of non-prescribing of anxiolytics in general practice. II: Factors associated with outcome. *British Journal of Psychiatry* **144**, 603–10.

——, ——, Edmonds, G., and Ennis, J. (1984*b*). The effects of non-prescribing of anxiolytics in general practice. I: Controlled evaluation of psychiatric and social outcome. *British Journal of Psychiatry* **144**, 593–602.

——, Hewett, J., Kennard, C., and McPherson, J. (1980*a*). The role of the nurse in the management of deliberate self-poisoning in the general hospital. *International Journal of nursing Studies* **17**, 275–82.

—— Marsack, P., Hawton, K. E., Whitwell, D., Fagg, J., and Bancroft, J. H. J. (1980*b*). Comparison of doctors and nurses in the assessment of deliberate self-poisoning patients. *Psychological Medicine* **10**, 483–91.

Central and Scottish Health Service Councils (1968). *Hospital treatment of acute poisoning*. HMSO, London.

Choquet, M., Facy F., and Davidson, F. (1980). Suicide and attempted suicide among adolescents in France. In *The suicide syndrome* (eds R. D. T. Farmer and S. Hirsch), pp. 73–89. Croom Helm, London.

Chowdhury, N., Hicks, R. C., and Kreitman, N. (1973). Evaluation of an aftercare service for parasuicide (attempted suicide) patients. *Social Psychiatry* **8**, 67–81.

—— and Kreitman, N. (1971). A comparison of parasuicides (attempted suicide) and the clients of the telephone Samaritan service. *Applied social Studies* **3**, 51–7.

Clare, A. W. (1983). Psychiatric and social aspects of premenstrual complaint. *Psychological Medicine*, Monograph Supplement Number 4.

Clendenin, W. W. and Murphy, G. E. (1971). Wrist-cutting: new epidemiological findings. *Archives of general Psychiatry* 25, 465–9.

Cohen, J. and Halpern, A. (1978). A practice counsellor. *Journal of the Royal College of general Practitioners* 28, 481–4.

Cooper, B., Harwin, B. G., Depla, C., and Shepherd, M. (1974). An experiment in community mental health care. *Lancet* ii, 1356–8.

Copas, J. B. and Robin, A. (1982). Suicide in psychiatric inpatients. *British Journal of Psychiatry* 141, 503–11.

Coppen, A., Abou-Saleh, M. T., Milln, P., Bailey, J., Metcalf, M., Burns, B. H., and Armond, A. (1981). Lithium continuation therapy following electroconvulsive therapy. *British Journal of Psychiatry* 139, 284–7.

Crammer, J. L. (1969). Poisoning and psychiatrists. *British medical Journal* iii, 651.

—— (1984). The special characteristics of suicide in hospital in-patients. *British Journal of Psychiatry* 145, 460–76.

—— Barraclough, B., and Heine, B. (1982). *The use of drugs in psychiatry*, 2nd edn. Gaskell, London.

Dalton, K. (1959). Menstruation and acute psychiatric illness. *British medical Journal* i, 148–9.

Davidson, D. G. D. and Eastham, W. N. (1966). Acute liver necrosis following overdose of paracetamol. *British medical Journal* ii, 497–9.

Davis, J. M. (1976). Overview: maintenance therapy in psychiatry. II Affective disorders. *American Journal of Psychiatry* 133, 1–13.

Department of Health and Social Security (1984). *The management of deliberate self-harm* HN (84) 25. Department of Health and Social Security, London.

Diekstra, R. F. W. (1985). Suicide and suicide attempts in the European Economic Community: an analysis of trends, with special emphasis upon trends among the young. *Suicide and life threatening Behaviour* 15, 27–42.

Dyer, J. A. T. and Kreitman, N. (1984). Hopelessness, depression and suicidal intent in parasuicide. *British Journal of Psychiatry* 144, 127–33.

Ebie, J. C. (1971). Features of psychiatric relevance at an experimental multi-disciplinary social casework centre in Edinburgh. *Social Psychiatry* 6, 122–8.

Eisenberg, L. (1980). Adolescent suicide: on taking arms against a sea of troubles. *Paediatrics* 66, 315–20.

Ettlinger, R. (1975). Evaluation of suicide prevention after attempted suicide *Acta psychiatrica Scandinavica*, Suppl. 260.

Evans, J. G. (1967). Deliberate self-poisoning in the Oxford area. *British Journal of preventive and social Medicine* 21, 97–107.

Ewing, C. P. (1978). *Crisis intervention as psychotherapy*. Oxford University Press, New York.

Falloon, I. R. H., Boyd, J. L., McGill, C. W., Razani, J., Moss, H. B., and Gilderman, A. M. (1982). Family management in the prevention of exacerbations of schizophrenia. *New England Journal of Medicine* 306, 1437–40.

Fernando, S. and Storm, V. (1984). Suicide among psychiatric patients of a district general hospital. *Psychological Medicine* 14, 661–72.

Forster, D. P. and Frost, C. E. B. (1985). Medicinal self-poisoning and prescription frequency. *Acta psychiatrica Scandinavica* 71, 657–74.

Fox, K. and Weissman, M. (1975). Suicide attempts and drugs: contradiction between method and intent. *Social Psychiatry* 10, 31–8.

Fox, R. (1975). The suicide drop—why? *Royal Society of Health Journal* 1, 9–20.

Freed, A. (1976). Prescribing of tranquillizers and barbiturates by general practitioners. *British medical Journal* ii, 1232–3.

Furnes, J. A., Khan, M. C., and Pickens, P. T. (1985). Unemployment and parasuicide in Hartlepool 1974–83. *Health Trends* 17, 21–4.

Gardner, A. R. and Gardner, A. J. (1975). Self-mutilation, obsessionality and narcissism. *British Journal of Psychiatry* 127, 127–32.

Gardner, R. Hanka, R., Evison, B., Mountford, P. M., O'Brien, V. C., and Roberts, S. J. (1978). Consultation-liaison scheme for self-poisoned patients in a general hospital. *British medical Journal* ii, 1392–4.

——, ——, O'Brien, V. C., Page, A. J. F., and Rees, R. (1977). Psychological and social evaluation in cases of deliberate self-poisoning admitted to a general hospital. *British medical Journal* ii, 1567–70.

Garfinkel, B. D. and Golombek, H. (1983). Suicide behaviour in adolescence. In *The adolescent and mood disturbance* (eds H. Golombek and B. D. Garfinkel), pp. 187–217. International Universities Press, New York.

Gazzard, B. G., Davis, M., Spooner, J., and Williams, R. (1976). Why do people use paracetamol for suicide? *British medical Journal* i, 212–3.

Ghodse, A. H. (1978). The attitudes of casualty staff and ambulance personnel towards patients who take drug overdoses. *Social Science and Medicine* 12A, 341–6.

—— (1979). Recommendations by accident and emergency staff about drug overdose patients. *Social Science and Medicine* 13A, 169–73.

Gibbons, J. L. (1979). *The Southampton parasuicide project*. Report to the DHSS, Department of Psychiatry, Royal South Hants Hospital, Southampton.

Gibbons, J. S., Butler, P., Urwin, P., and Gibbons, J. L. (1978a). Evaluation of a social work service for self-poisoning patients. *British Journal of Psychiatry* 133, 111–18.

——, Elliot, J., Urwin, P., and Gibbons, J. L. (1978b). The urban environment and deliberate self-poisoning: trends in Southampton 1972–77. *Social Psychiatry* 13, 159–66.

Ginsburg, G. P. (1971). Public conceptions and attitudes about suicide. *Journal of Health and social Behaviour* 12, 200–7.

Graff, H. and Mallin, R. (1967). The syndrome of the wrist cutter. *American Journal of Psychiatry* 124, 36–42.

Green, A. M. (1978). Self-destructive behavior in battered children. *American Journal of Psychiatry* 135, 579–82.

Greer, S. and Bagley, C. (1971). Effect of psychiatric intervention in attempted suicide: a controlled study. *British medical Journal* i, 310–2.

Hawton, K. (1978). Deliberate self-poisoning and self-injury in the psychiatric hospital. *British Journal of medical Psychology* 51, 253–9.

—— (1982). How patients and psychiatrists account for overdoses. In *Personal meanings* (eds E. Shepherd and J. Watson), pp. 103–14. Wiley, Chichester.

—— (1986). *Suicide and attempted suicide among children and adolescents.* Sage, Beverley Hills.

——, Bancroft, J., Catalan, J., Kingston, B., Stedeford, A., and Welch, N. (1981a). Domiciliary and out-patient treatment of self-poisoning patients by medical and non-medical staff. *Psychological Medicine* 11, 169–77.

——, ——, and Simkin, S. (1978a). Attitudes of psychiatric patients to deliberate self-poisoning. *British Journal of Psychiatry* 132, 31–5.

—— and Blackstock, E. (1976). General practice aspects of self-poisoning and self-injury. *Psychological Medicine* 6, 571–5.

——, Crowle, J., Simkin, S., and Bancroft, J. (1978b). Attempted suicide and suicide among Oxford University students. *British Journal of Psychiatry* 132, 506–9.

—— and Fagg, J. Suicide and other causes of death following attempted suicide. (In preparation.)

——, ——, and Marsack, P. (1980). Association between epilepsy and attempted suicide. *Journal of Neurology, Neurosurgery and Psychiatry* 43, 168–70.

——, ——, Marsack, P., and Wells, P. (1982a). Deliberate self-poisoning and self-injury in the Oxford area: 1972–80. *Social Psychiatry* 17, 175–9.

——, ——, and Simkin, S. Unemployment and attempted suicide among women in Oxford. (In preparation.)

——, Gath, D. H., and Smith, E. B. O. (1979). Management of attempted suicide in Oxford. *British medical Journal* ii, 1040–2.

—— and Goldacre, M. (1982). Hospital admissions for adverse effects of medicinal agents (mainly self-poisoning) among adolescents in the Oxford region. *British Journal of Psychiatry* 141, 166–70.

——, Marsack, P., and Fagg, J. (1981b). The attitudes of psychiatrists to deliberate self-poisoning: comparison with· physicians and nurses. *British Journal of medical Psychology* 54, 341–7.

——, McKeown, S., Day, A., Martin, P., O'Connor, M., and Yule, J.

(1987). Evaluation of outpatient counselling compared with general practitioner care following overdoses. *Psychological Medicine* (in press).

——, O'Grady, J., Osborn, M., and Cole, D. (1982*b*). Adolescents who take overdoses: their characteristics, problems and contacts with helping agencies. *British Journal of Psychiatry* **140**, 118–23.

——, Osborn, M., O'Grady, J., and Cole, D. (1982*c*). Classification of adolescents who take overdoses. *British Journal of Psychiatry* **140**, 124–31.

——, Roberts, J., and Goodwin, G. (1985). The risk of child abuse among attempted suicide mothers with young children. *British Journal of Psychiatry* **146**, 486–9.

—— and Rose, N. (1986). Unemployment and attempted suicide among men in Oxford. *Health Trends* **18**, 29–32.

Holding, T. (1974). The BBC 'Befrienders' series and its effects. *British Journal of Psychiatry* **124**, 470–2.

——, Buglass, D., Duffy, J. C., and Kreitman, N. (1977). Parasuicide in Edinburgh—a seven year review 1968–74. *British Journal of Psychiatry* **130**, 534–43.

Jacobs, G. (1971). *Adolescent suicide*. Wiley-Interscience, New York.

Jacobsen, E. (1938). *Progressive relaxation*. University of Chicago Press.

James, D. and Hawton, K. (1985). Overdoses: explanations and attitudes in self-poisoners and significant others. *British Journal of Psychiatry* **146**, 481–5.

Jennings, C., Barraclough, B. M., and Moss, J. R. (1978). Have the Samaritans lowered the suicide rate? A controlled study. *Psychological Medicine* **8**, 413–22.

Johnson, D. A. W. (1973). Treatment of depression in general practice. *British medical Journal* ii, 18–20.

Johnston, M. (1978). The work of a clinical psychologist in primary care. *Journal of the Royal College of general Practitioners* **29**, 661–7.

Johnstone, E., Lawler, P., Stevens, M., Deakin, J. F. W., Frith, C. D., McPherson, K., and Crow, T. J. (1980). The Northwick Park electroconvulsive therapy trial. *Lancet* ii, 1317–20.

Jones, D. I. R. (1977). Self-poisoning with drugs: the past 20 years in Sheffield. *British medical Journal* i, 28–9.

Kendell, R. E. (1981). The present status of electroconvulsive therapy. *British Journal of Psychiatry* **139**, 265–83.

Kennedy, P. (1972). Efficacy of a regional poisoning treatment centre in preventing further suicidal behaviour. *British medical Journal* iv, 255–7.

—— and Kreitman, N. (1973). An epidemiological survey of parasuicide (attempted suicide) in general practice. *British Journal of Psychiatry* **123**, 23–34.

Kessel, N. (1965). Self-poisoning. *British medical Journal* ii, 1265–70, 1336–40.

—— (1985). Patients who take overdoses. *British medical Journal* 290, 1297–8.

—— and McCulloch, W. (1966). Repeated acts of self-poisoning and self-injury. *Proceedings of the Royal Society of Medicine* 59, 89–92.

Kingston, B. and Hawton, K. (1977). Another paracetamol tragedy. *Nursing Times* 73, 272.

Kobler, A. L. and Stotland, E. (1964). *The end of hope.* The Free Press, New York.

Koller, K. and Slaghuis, W. (1978). Suicide attempts 1973–77—urban Hobart. A further five year follow-up reporting a decline. *Australian and New Zealand Journal of Psychiatry* 12, 169–73.

Koocher, P. G. (1974). Talking with children about death. *American Journal of Orthopsychiatry* 44, 404–11.

Kosky, R. (1982). Suicide and attempted suicide among Australian children. *Medical Journal of Australia* i, 124–6.

Kreitman, N. (ed.) (1977). *Parasuicide.* John Wiley, London.

—— (1979). Reflections on the management of parasuicide. *British Journal of Psychiatry* 135, 275–7.

—— (1980). Services for parasuicide and the place of the poisonings unit. In *The suicide syndrome* (eds R. Farmer and S. Hirsch) pp. 259–62. Croom Helm, London.

—— and Chowdhury, N. (1973*a*). Distress behaviour: a study of selected Samaritan clients and parasuicides ('attempted suicide' patients). Part I: general aspects. *British Journal of Psychiatry* 123, 1–8.

—— and —— (1973*b*). Distress behaviour: a study of selected Samaritan clients and parasuicides ('attempted suicide' patients). Part II: Attitudes and choice of action. *British Journal of Psychiatry* 123, 9–14.

——, Philip, A. E., Greer, S., and Bagley, C. R. (1969). Parasuicide. *British Journal of Psychiatry* 115, 746–7.

Kushner, A. W. (1967). Two cases of auto-castration due to religious delusions. *British Journal of medical Psychology* 40, 293–8.

Langley, G. E. and Bayatti, N. N. (1984). Suicides in Exe Vale Hospital, 1972–1981. *British Journal of Psychiatry* 145, 463–7.

Lawson, A. A. H. and Mitchell, I. (1972). Patients with acute poisoning seen in a general medical unit (1960–71). *British medical Journal* iv, 153–6.

Leach, R. H. and White, P. L. (1978). Use and wastage of prescribed medicines in the home. *Journal of the Royal College of general Practitioners* 28, 32–6.

Leff, J., Kuipers, L., Berkowitz, R., Eberlein-Vries, R., and Sturgeon, D. (1982). A controlled trial of social intervention in the families of schizophrenic patients. *British Journal of Psychiatry* 141, 121–34.

——, ——, ——, and Sturgeon, D. (1985). A controlled trial of social intervention in the families of schizophrenic patients: two year follow-up. *British Journal of Psychiatry* **146**, 594–600.

Lennard-Jones, J. E. and Asher, R. C. (1959). Why do they do it? A study of pseudocide. *Lancet* i, 1138–40.

Lester, D. (1974). Effect of suicide prevention centres on suicide rates in the United States. *Health Service Reports* **89**, 37–9.

—— and Murrell, M. E. (1980). The influence of gun control laws on suicidal behaviour. *American Journal of Psychiatry* **137**, 121–2.

Levy, S. and Southcombe, R. H. (1953). Suicide in a state hospital for the mentally ill. *Journal of nervous and mental disease* **117**, 504–14.

Liberman, R. P. and Eckman, T. (1981). Behaviour therapy *vs.* insight-oriented therapy for repeated suicide attempters. *Archives of general Psychiatry* **38**, 1126–30.

Mackay, A. (1979). Self-poisoning—a complication of epilepsy. *British Journal of Psychiatry* **134**, 277–82.

Marsh, G. N. and Barr, J. (1975). Marriage guidance counselling in a group practice. *Journal of the Royal College of general Practitioners* **25**, 73–5.

Matthew, H., Proudfoot, A. T., Brown, S. S., and Aitken, R. C. B. (1969). Acute poisoning: organization and work-load of a treatment centre. *British medical Journal* iii, 489–93.

Mayfield, D., McLeod, G., and Hall, P. (1974). The CAGE questionnaire: validation of a new alcoholism screening instrument. *American Journal of Psychiatry* **131**, 1121–3.

McCulloch, J. W. and Philip, A. E. (1967). Social variables in attempted suicide. *Acta psychiatrica Scandinavica* **43**, 341–6.

McKerracher, D. W., Loughnane, T., and Watson, R. A. (1968). Self-mutilation in female psychopaths. *British Journal of Psychiatry* **114**, 829–32.

Miller, H. L., Coombs, D. W., Leeper, J. D., and Barton, S. N. (1984). An analysis of the effects of suicide prevention facilities on suicide rates in the United States. *Journal of public Health* **74**, 340–3.

Ministry of Health (1961). HM Circular (61), 94, London.

Minkoff, K. Bergman, E., Beck, A. T., and Beck, R. (1973). Hopelessness, depression and attempted suicide. *American Journal of Psychiatry* **130**, 455–9.

Montgomery, S. A., Montgomery, D. B., Rani, S. J., Roy, D. N., Shaw, P. J., and McAvley, R. (1979). Maintenance therapy in repeat suicidal behaviour: a placebo controlled trial. In *Proceedings communication: 10th International congress for suicide prevention and crisis intervention, Ottawa,* 17–20 June, 1979.

Morgan, H. G. (1979). *Death wishes? The understanding and management of deliberate self-harm.* John Wiley, Chichester.

——, Barton, J., Pottle, S., Pocock, H., and Burns-Cox, C. J. (1976).

Deliberate self-harm: a follow-up study of 279 patients. *British Journal of Psychiatry* **128**, 361–8.

——, Burns-Cox, C. J., Pocock, H., and Pottle, S. (1975*a*). Deliberate self-harm: clinical and socio-economic characteristics of 368 patients. *British Journal of Psychiatry* **126**, 564–74.

——, Pocock, H., and Pottle, S. (1975*b*). The urban distribution of non-fatal deliberate self-harm. *British Journal of Psychiatry* **126**, 319–28.

—— and Priest, P. (1984). Assessment of suicide risk in psychiatric in-patients. *British Journal of Psychiatry* **145**, 467–9.

Murphy, G. E. (1984). The prediction of suicide: why is it so difficult? *American Journal of Psychotherapy* **38**, 341–9.

Nelson, S. H. and Grunebaum, H. (1971). A follow-up study of wrist-slashers. *American Journal of Psychiatry* **127**, 1345–9.

Newson-Smith, J. G. B. and Hirsch, S. R. (1979*a*). Psychiatric symptoms in self-poisoning patients. *Psychological Medicine* **9**, 493–500.

—— and —— (1979*b*). A comparison of social workers and psychiatrists in evaluating parasuicide. *British Journal of Psychiatry* **134**, 335–42.

Nielsen, J. and Videbech, T. (1973). Suicide frequency before and after introduction of community psychiatry in a Danish island. *British Journal of Psychiatry* **123**, 35–9.

Office of Health Economics (1981). *Suicide and deliberate self-harm.* London.

Ovenstone, I. M. K. (1973). Spectrum of suicidal behaviours in Edinburgh. *British Journal of preventive and social Medicine* **27**, 27–35.

—— and Kreitman, N. (1974). Two syndromes of suicide. *British Journal of Psychiatry* **124**, 336–45.

Pallis, D. J. (1984. *Estimating suicide risk among attempted suicides: guidelines for the administration and predictive efficiency of Post-Attempt Risk Assessment (para-suicide) scales.* MRC Clinical Psychiatry Unit, Graylingwell Hospital, Chichester.

—— and Barraclough, B. M. (1977). Seriousness of suicide attempt and future risk of suicide: a comment on Card's paper. *Omega* **8**, 141–9.

——, ——, Levey, A. B., Jenkins, J. S., and Sainsbury, P. (1982). Estimating suicide risk among attempted suicides: I. The development of new clinical scales. *British Journal of Psychiatry* **141**, 37–44.

——, Gibbons, J. S., and Pierce, D. W. (1984). Estimating suicide risk among attempted suicides: II, Efficiency of predictive scales after the attempt. *British Journal of Psychiatry* **144**, 139–48.

—— and Sainsbury, P. (1976). The value of assessing intent in attempted suicide. *Psychological Medicine* **6**, 487–92.

Parrish, H. M. (1957). Epidemiology of suicide among college students. *Yale Journal of Biology and Medicine* **29**, 585–95.

Parry-Jones, W. (1973). Criminal law and complicity in suicide and attempted suicide. *Medicine, Science and the Law* **13**, 110–19.

Patel, A. R. (1975). Attitudes towards self-poisoning, *British medical Journal* ii, 426–30.

Paykel, E. S., Prusoff, B. A., and Myers, J. K. (1975). Suicide attempts and recent life events: a controlled comparison. *Archives of general Psychiatry* 32, 327–33.

Perry, A. and Tsuang, M. T. (1979). Treatment of unipolar depression following electroconvulsive therapy. *Journal of affective Disorders* 1, 123–9.

Peterson, L. G., Peterson, M., O'Sharrick, G. J., and Swann, A. (1985). Self-inflicted gunshot wounds: lethality of method versus intent. *American Journal of Psychiatry* 142, 228–31.

Piaget, J. (1960). *The child's concept of the world.* Littlefield Adams, Patterson, New York.

Pierce, D. (1984). Suicidal intent and repeated self-harm. *Psychological Medicine* 14, 655–9.

Pierce, D. W. (1981). Predictive validation of a suicide intent scale. *British Journal of Psychiatry* 139, 391–6.

Pitts, F. N. and Winokur, G. (1964). Affective disorders III: diagnostic correlates and incidence of suicide. *Journal of nervous and mental Disease* 139, 176–81.

Platt, S., Hawton, K., Fagg, J., and Kreitman, N. Trends in parasuicide in Edinburgh and Oxford, 1976–1984. (In preparation.)

—— and Kreitman, N. (1984). Trends in parasuicide and unemployment among men in Edinburgh, 1968–82. *British medical Journal* 289, 1029–32.

—— and —— (1985a). Is unemployment a cause of parasuicide? *British medical Journal* 290, 161.

—— and —— (1985b). Suicide and unemployment among men in Edinburgh 1968–82. *Psychological Medicine* 15, 113–23.

Pokorny, A. D. (1964). Suicide rate in various psychiatric disorders. *Journal of nervous and mental Disease* 139, 499–506.

Post, R. M. (1982). Use of the anticonvulsant carbamazepine in primary and secondary affective illness: clinical and theoretical implications. *Psychological Medicine* 12, 701–4.

Power, K. G., Cooke, D. L., and Brooks, D. N. (1985). Life stress, medical lethality, and suicidal intent. *British Journal of Psychiatry* 147, 655–9.

Prescott, L. F. and Highley, M. S. (1985). Drugs prescribed for self-poisoners. *British medical Journal* 290, 1633–6.

Proudfoot, A. T. and Park. J. (1978). Changing pattern of drugs used for self-poisoning. *British medical Journal* i, 90–3.

Puzynski, S. and Klosiewicz, L. (1984). Valproic acid amide in the treatment of affective and schizoaffective disorders. *Journal of affective Disorders* 6, 115–21.

Ramon, S., Bancroft, J. H. J., and Skrimshire, A. M. (1975). Attitudes towards self-poisoning among physicians and nurses in a general hospital. *British Journal of Psychiatry* **127**, 257–64.

Reid, W. and Epstein, L. (1972). *Task-centred casework*, Columbia University press.

Richman, J. (1979). The family therapy of attempted suicide. *Family Process* **18**, 131–42.

Roberts, J. and Hawton, K. (1980). Child abuse and attempted suicide. *British Journal of Psychiatry* **137**, 319–23.

Robins, E., Murphy, G. E., Wilkinson, R. H., Gassner, S., and Kays, J. (1959). Some clinical considerations in prevention of suicide based on a study of 134 successful suicides. *American Journal of public Health* **49**, 888–99.

Robson, M., France, R., and Bland, M. (1984). Clinical psychologists in primary care: controlled clinical and economic evaluation. *British medical Journal* **288**, 1805–8.

Rohn, R. D., Sarles, R. M., Kenny, T. J., Reynolds, B. J., and Head, F. P. (1977). Adolescents who attempt suicide. *Journal of Paediatrics* **90**, 636–8.

Rosen, B. K. (1981). Suicide pacts: a review. *Psychological Medicine* **11**, 525–33.

Rosen, L. W. and Thomas, M. A. (1984). Treatment techniques for chronic wrist cutters. *Journal of behaviour Therapy and experimental Psychiatry* **141**, 520–5.

Rosenthal, P. A. and Rosenthal, S. (1984). Suicidal behavior by preschool children. *American Journal of Psychiatry* **141**, 520–5.

Rosenthal, R. J., Rinzler, C., Wallsh, R., and Klausner, E. (1972). Wrist-cutting syndrome: the meaning of a gesture. *American Journal of Psychiatry* **128**, 1363–8.

Ross, C. P. (1986). School and suicide: Education for life and death. In *Adolescent suicide* (eds R. Diekstra and K. Hawton). Martinus Nijhoff, Dordrecht.

Roy, A. (1982). Risk factors for suicide in psychiatric patients. *Archives of general Psychiatry* **39**, 1089–95.

Royal College of Psychiatrists (1977). The Royal College of Psychiatrists' memorandum on the use of electroconvulsive therapy. *British Journal of Psychiatry* **131**, 261–72.

—— (1982). The management of parasuicide in young people under sixteen. *Bulletin of the Royal College of Psychiatrists* **6**, 182–5.

Ryerson, D. M. (1986). 'ASAP'—an adolescent suicide awareness program. In *Adolescent suicide* (eds R. Kiekstra and K. Hawton). Martinus Nijhoff, Dordrecht.

Saghir, M. T. and Robins, E. (1973). *Male and female homosexuality: a comprehensive investigation*. Williams and Wilkins, Baltimore.

Sainsbury, P. (1973). Suicide: opinions and facts. *Proceedings of the Royal Society of Medicine* 66, 9–17.

Sale, I., Williams, C., Clark, J., and Mills, J. (1975). Suicide behaviour: community attitudes and beliefs. *Suicide* 5, 158–68.

Salmons, P. H. (1984). Suicide in high buildings. *British Journal of Psychiatry* 145, 469–72.

Shaffer, D. and Fisher, P. (1981). The epidemiology of suicide in children and adolescents. *Journal of the American Academy of child Psychiatry* 20, 545–65.

Shapiro, C. M. and Parry, M. R. (1984). Is unemployment a cause of parasuicide? *British medical Journal* 289, 1622.

Shepherd, M., Harwin, B. G., Depla, C., and Cairns, V. (1979). Social work and the primary care of mental disorder. *Psychological Medicine* 9, 661–9.

Simpson, M. A. (1975). The phenomenology of self-mutilation in a general hospital setting. *Canadian Psychiatric Association Journal* 20, 429–33.

—— (1976). Self-mutilation. *British Journal of hospital Medicine* 16, 430–8.

Skegg, D. C. G., Doll, R., and Perry, J. (1977). Use of medicines in general practice. *British medical Journal* i, 1561–3.

Skegg, K., Skegg, D. C. G., and Richards, S. M. (1983). Incidence of self-poisoning in patients prescribed psychotropic drugs. *British medical Journal* 286, 841–3.

Skrimshire, A. M. (1976). A small area analysis of self-poisoning and self-injury in the region of Oxford. *Journal of biosocial Science* 8, 85–112.

Smith, A. J. (1972). Self-poisoning with drugs: a worsening situation. *British medical Journal* iv, 157–9.

Smith, J. S. and Davison, K. (1971). Changes in the pattern of admission for attempted suicide in Newcastle-upon-Tyne during the 1960s. *British medical Journal* iv, 412–15.

Smith, R. (1985a). Occupationless health. 'What's the point. I'm no use to anybody': the psychological consequences of unemployment. *British medical Journal* 291, 1338–41.

—— (1985b). Occupationless health. 'I couldn't stand it any more': suicide and unemployment. *British medical Journal* 291, 1563–6.

Stanley, W. J. (1969). Attempted suicide and suicidal gestures. *British Journal of preventive and social Medicine* 23, 190–5.

Stengel, E. and Cook, N. G. (1958). *Attempted suicide: its social significance and effects.* Maudsley Monograph Number Four, Oxford University Press, London.

Stuart, R. B. (1980). *Helping couples change: a social learning approach to marital therapy.* Guilford Press, New York.

Taylor, E. A. and Stansfield, S. A. (1984). Children who poison themselves:

I. Clinical comparison with psychiatric controls, and II. Prediction of attendance for treatment. *British Journal of Psychiatry* **145**, 127–35.

Temple, S. amd Catalan, J. (1977). Group work with patients following deliberate self-poisoning or self-injury. *Occupational Therapy* **40**, 306–8.

Termansen, P. E. and Bywater, C. (1975). S.A.F.E.R. A follow-up service for attempted suicide. *Canadian Psychiatric Association Journal* **20**, 29–34.

Tonks, C. M., Rack, P. H., and Rose, M. J. (1968). Attempted suicide and the menstrual cycle. *Journal of psychosomatic Research* **11**, 319–23.

Trautman, E. C. (1961). The suicidal fit. *Archives of general Psychiatry* **5**, 98–105.

Tuckman, J. and Youngman, W. F. (1968). A scale for assessing suicide risk of attempted suicides. *Journal of clinical Psychology* **24**, 17–19.

Urwin, P. and Gibbons, J. L. (1979). Psychiatric diagnosis in self-poisoning patients. *Psychological Medicine* **9**, 501–7.

Vaughn, C. E. and Leff, J. P. (1976). The influence of family and social factors on the course of psychiatric illness: a comparison of schizophrenic and depressed neurotic patients. *British Journal of Psychiatry* **129**, 125–37.

Walk, D. (1967). Suicide and community care. *British Journal of Psychiatry* **113**, 1381–91.

Walker, W. L. (1980). Intentional self-injury in school age children. *Journal of Adolescence* **3**, 217–28.

Walsh, B. W. and Rosen, P. R. (1985). Self-mutilation and contagion: an empircal test. *American Journal of Psychiatry* **142**, 119–20.

Weiner, I. W. (1969). The effectiveness of a suicide prevention program. *Mental Hygiene* **53**, 357–6.

Weissman, M. M. (1974). The epidemiology of suicide attempts, 1960 to 1971. *Archives of general Psychiatry* **30**, 737–46.

—— (1975). Wrist cutting: relationship between clinical observations and epidemiological findings. *Archives of general Psychiatry* **32**, 1166–71.

Welu, T. C. (1977). A follow-up program for suicide attempters: evaluation of effectiveness. *Suicide and life threatening Behavior* **7**, 17–30.

Wetzel, R. D. (1976). Hopelessness, depression and suicide intent. *Archives of general Psychiatry* **33**, 1069–73.

——, Margulies, T., Davis, R., and Karam, E. (1980). Hopelessness, depression and suicidal intent. *Journal of clinical Psychiatry* **41**, 159–60.

Wexler, L., Weissman, M. M., and Kasl, S. V. (1978). Suicide attempts 1970–75: updating a United States study and comparisons with international trends. *British Journal of Psychiatry* **132**, 180–5.

White, H. C. (1974). Self-poisoning in adolescents. *British Journal of*

Psychiatry **124**, 24–35.

Whitehead, P. C., Johnson, F. G., and Ferrence, R. (1973). Measuring the incidence of self-injury: some methodological and design considerations. *American Journal of Orthopsychiatry* **43**, 142–8.

Wing, J. K., Cooper, J. E., and Sartorius, N. (1974). *The measurement and classification of psychiatric symptoms*. Cambridge University Press, London.

Index